T0374370

Leadership Fatigue
What New Leaders Can Learn from an Old King

Carlo A. Serrano, Ph.D.

WESTBOW
PRESS®
A DIVISION OF THOMAS NELSON
& ZONDERVAN

Copyright © 2017 Carlo A. Serrano, Ph.D.

All rights reserved. No part of this book may be used or reproduced by any means,
graphic, electronic, or mechanical, including photocopying, recording, taping or by
any information storage retrieval system without the written permission of the author
except in the case of brief quotations embodied in critical articles and reviews.

WestBow Press books may be ordered through booksellers or by contacting:

WestBow Press
A Division of Thomas Nelson & Zondervan
1663 Liberty Drive
Bloomington, IN 47403
www.westbowpress.com
1 (866) 928-1240

Because of the dynamic nature of the Internet, any web addresses or links contained
in this book may have changed since publication and may no longer be valid. The views
expressed in this work are solely those of the author and do not necessarily reflect the
views of the publisher, and the publisher hereby disclaims any responsibility for them.

Any people depicted in stock imagery provided by Thinkstock are models,
and such images are being used for illustrative purposes only.
Certain stock imagery © Thinkstock.

The Holy Bible, English Standard Version® (ESV®)
Copyright © 2001 by Crossway, a publishing ministry of Good News Publishers.
All rights reserved. ESV Text Edition: 2016

ISBN: 978-1-9736-0254-5 (sc)
ISBN: 978-1-9736-0255-2 (hc)
ISBN: 978-1-9736-0253-8 (e)

Library of Congress Control Number: 2017913494

Print information available on the last page.

WestBow Press rev. date: 8/28/2017

Dedication

This work is dedicated to my primary sources of motivation: Jaemi, Tony, and David. Jaemi, you have always brought out the best in me and pushed me to believe in my God-given potential. Thank you for your sacrifice, endless love, and inspiration. I have not stopped falling in love with you! Tony, thank you for being a leader, a great big brother, and an honorable son. You are dearly loved. Never stop learning. David, thank you for putting up with my long work days and for helping me study for my comprehensive exams. You are dearly loved. Never stop learning. The greatest joy of my life is watching you three grow in grace. Our family is a testimony to the final statement of this book: there is always room for redemption.

"Now, to Him who has kept me from stumbling through this entire process, to the only wise God, my savior, be glory, majesty, dominion, and power both now and forever. Amen" (Jude 24-25).

Acknowledgements

A project as intensive as this does not happen in isolation. I must give credit to my friends, family, and colleagues for the critical role they played in this study. However, I must first thank my Lord and our Savior, Jesus Christ, for saving me, calling me, and equipping me to serve His people as a pastor–teacher. May I never forget your grace and truth. Help me to love, lead, and learn from a posture of humility. May every project I do in your name lead to life change. Amen.

I would like to thank my wife, Jaemi, and our sons, Tony and David, for their sacrifice and patience during this process. To my brothers and sisters—Eddie, Nate, Sylvia, and Stephanie—thank you for supporting me and always having my back. I also would like to thank John and Laurie Johnson for being the world's greatest in-laws. I love you! Finally, I am not the man I am today without the guidance and love of my parents, Frank and Pearl Serrano. I know they are cheering me on with the great cloud of witnesses (Hebrews 12:1).

I am forever indebted to the wonderful faculty and staff of the Regent University School of Business and Leadership. I want to give a special thanks to my mentor throughout this process, Dr. Joshua Henson. Thank you for shepherding me with patience, grace, and just the right amount of push! I would also like to acknowledge Dr. Bruce Winston and Dr. Doris Gomez for not only advising me during this project, but for their outstanding service to me during the coursework phase of my doctoral program. To Dr. Kathleen Patterson, thank you for being a great example of servant leadership in action! Finally, to Dr. Corné Bekker, thank you for being a loving pastor and attentive instructor to your students. Lead on!

I am thankful that I got to be a part of the Fall 2013 Ph.D. cohort at

Regent University. Although we did not have a residency requirement, we found a way to connect and walk through the program together. Robert Huizinga, Doreen O'Connor, Kamerin Lauren, and Matthew Chadwick, thank you for your prayers, text messages, hangouts, and always *on time* Facebook humor! I would also like to thank my dear friends—Dr. Steve Estep, Dr. Steven Crowther, Dr. Ken Gilman, Dr. Aaron Allison, Pastor Tom Johnson, Ron McBride, Pastor Mike Burnette, Pastor Chris Edmondson, and Tim Catchim—for always being willing to *talk shop* with me. Every man needs a band of brothers, and I am honored to call you my tribe. To the wonderful people of GraceLife Church and oneChurch.tv, thank you for giving me the space to grow as a leader and scholar. We are better together!

Special Thanks

The book in your hands would not be there if it were not for Angie Terrado of More than Words Therapy Services, LLC (MTW). A doctoral research project is a time intensive labor of love. Thousands of dissertations and theses never see the light of day once the approving committees gives their seal approval. Thanks to the generosity of Angie and MTW, my passion for the life and leadership of King David will live beyond my doctoral dissertation!

MTW provides quality therapy to children and their families in Clarksville, TN and in the Ft. Campbell/Oak Grove, KY areas. What sets MTW apart from other therapy providers is that they take pride in: involving caregivers into therapy routines, partnering with parents, and finding innovative ways to provide therapy that keeps their patients engaged from beginning to end. This family and military friendly organization leads the way in modeling ethical and moral leadership! Thank you Angie and MTW!

Contents

INTRODUCTION

The General Has Fallen

"Here comes the General!"[1], shouted my squad leader. My five man team jumped out of our seats to the position of attention and waited for the door to open in our rare, air conditioned trailer. "ATTENTION!" boomed some random Captain who happened to be escorting the General that day. The door swung open and in walked my hero, the scholar, the statesman, the warrior's warrior and future Director of the Central Intelligence Agency (CIA): Major General David H. Petraeus. In the summer of 2003, I was four months into a deployment with the famed *Screaming Eagles* of the 101st Airborne Division (Air Assault) in support of Operation Iraqi Freedom. In the springtime when kings go off to war, I left behind a pregnant wife and my young son and joined tens of thousands of troops who were headed off to fight in Babylon...again. I will never forget the smell, the heat, the noise, and the uncertainty that gripped us all as we moved from camp to camp in Kuwait, and eventually *across the berm* into Saddam's Iraq.[2] On March 19, 2003 Gen. Petraeus issued the following radio message: "Guidons guidons! This is Eagle 6. The 101st Airborne Division's next Rendezvous with Destiny is North to Baghdad, Op-Ord Desert Eagle 2 is now in effect. Godspeed. Air Assault. Out" (Broadwell & Loeb, 2012, "Lines of Operation," para. 56). With those words, the already well-known General accelerated his rise to the top.

Gen. Petraeus went on to lead at the highest levels of military command and literally wrote the manual for Counter-insurgency operations. However,

---

[1] Also a great line from the musical Hamilton by Lin-Manuel Miranda!

[2] Due to an emergency situation at home, I did not invade Iraq until late April 2003.

on that hot summer day in 2003, he was our leader, the one we looked to for guidance, and the one we had hoped would give us good news regarding the length of our deployment. The General walked into our trailer and greeted us all by (last) name, asked us where we were from, and then shared with us how lucky we were to have one of the first air conditioned trailer-workspaces in the area of operation. He also broke the news to us that we would be in Iraq for at least 12 months. I will never forget how he looked each of us in the eyes and shared with us that he too had not seen his family for several months. He showed great leadership and empathy that day and forever won my respect. I saw Gen. Petraeus several more times after that during the deployment and I will always cherish the honor of having served in combat under his leadership...even after August 15th, 2015.

On that date, my hero, the scholar, the statesman, and the warrior's warrior plead guilty to charges of mishandling classified information. The entire ordeal was precipitated by the exposure of an extramarital affair the General had with his biographer, all of which had been in the media since the fall of 2012. When I heard the news I actually became quite emotional. My heart broke for all who were involved. However, what pained me the most is that I had no real answer for how a great leader could fall so hard, so fast. The General had fallen and I wished it were not so. It is no secret that leaders in all arenas experience ethical and moral failure. However, this one bothered me to the core. So, when I began my doctoral studies at Regent University I went in knowing that eventually, I wanted to study the phenomenon of leadership failure.

Both my Bachelor's in Psychology and my Master's in Pastoral Counseling prepared me to explore the psychosocial complexities of life and leadership in military contexts. Furthermore, in the fall of 2012 I helped start a non-profit organization designed to help soldiers and their families deal with the stress of military life both at home and *down-range* through a series of weekend retreats. During these retreats, we walk the soldiers and their families through the life of another great military leader. In fact, this man was more than a military man. He was a father, a warrior, and one of history's most storied political leaders: King David of Israel. It was not until after I finished my doctoral dissertation that I realized the similarities between General David Petraeus and King David. Both were proven warriors on the battlefield, both were well-loved and respected by broad audiences, both led their organizations to new heights of success, and both were brought down by political scandal involving a woman. How does that happen? Why does that happen? Although it is beyond the scope of this volume to explore the life and leadership of David Petraeus, I will answer these questions by exploring the life of King David of Israel.

Let me be clear: this is not a novel or an opinion-piece. This book is the result of years of undergraduate, graduate, and doctoral level qualitative research and preparation. My hope is that it will be beneficial to current leaders and scholars as well as future leaders who are currently exploring the broad field of organizational leadership in classrooms and libraries all over the world. I believe that the research presented in this book helps to confirm that the Bible is an appropriate source for organizational leadership research. Moreover, I believe that this book will help the leader who is tired, on-edge, and ready to throw it all away for one night of temporary release. Leadership is hard and traumatic...we must deal with it.

If you are reading this and you just want to get to the bottom line principles, you can probably get away with reading the Introduction, Chapter 1, Chapter 12, and the Conclusion. If you are student of leadership, I believe that you will find Chapters 1, 2, and 11 to be very informative. If you are a student of the Hebrew and Christian scriptures, I encourage you to take your time reading Chapters 3 through 5. In those Chapters you will find a strong argument for the efficacy of Scripture in research as well as a crash-course in sociorhetorical analysis. Finally, no matter who you are, I hope that you will mindfully walk through Chapters 6 through 10. This book centers on what I believe is a serious mediating factor in unethical and immoral decision-making: Leadership Fatigue. I know the language may get a bit dense at times but again, this is a scholarly text with powerful and practical implications. Lead on!

CHAPTER 1

Leadership: It's All About Ethics

The world needs ethical and moral leaders. Even a casual look into the political arena, military command, and even religious institutions reveals an ever-increasing turn toward ethical and moral failure in organizational leadership. An increase in scandals and ethical failures highlights the fact that although many organizations have implemented training to prevent ethical failure, failure continues to occur at an alarming rate (De Cremer, Tenbrunsel, & Dijke, 2010). Not to mention, studies have suggested that few Americans trust the ethical leadership, morality, and integrity of the nation's top leaders due to the prevalence of unethical decision making and behavior (Brown & Treviño, 2014; Schaubroek et al., 2002; Zheng et al., 2015).

Kouzes and Posner (2006) argued that the primary function of leadership is to *model the way* for followers. If leaders are modeling unethical and immoral behavior, one could assume that followers may follow suit. Hoyt and Price (2015) argued, "One source of moral failure in group life stems from people deviating from moral requirements to help their group attain its goals" (p. 531). In view of the *pervasiveness* of ethical leadership failure, it is important for both scholars and practitioners to work together to exhaustively search for robust and practical solutions that will reverse the trend of ethical and moral failure in organizational leadership (De Cremer et al., 2010, p. 1; Midgen, 2015).

As a discipline, leadership has been broadly defined, practically applied, and explored on multiple levels with an increasing emphasis on how morality and ethics influence effective leadership. According to Patterson (2003), the virtuous theory of servant leadership depends upon moral character and manifests in moral (*agapao*) love. Avolio and Gardner (2005) suggested that authentic leadership contains an inherent moral and ethical component. Burns (1978) argued that moral leadership is more than just *talking* about what is right; it is *being* and *doing* what is right to the extent that the authentic needs of followers are met in a way that produces positive social change.

According to Bass (2009), a leader may be "moral in beliefs and ethical in behavior; they may be amoral in beliefs and neutral in behavior; or they may be immoral in beliefs and unethical in behavior" (p. 205). Likewise, Fry (2003) argued that spiritual leadership inspires ethical behavior in followers because of the moral imperatives found within ethical systems. Thus, there appears to be a strong connection between ethical and moral leadership in the developmental progression of values-based leadership theories such as servant leadership, authentic leadership, transformational leadership, and spiritual leadership. In fact, Ciulla (1995) proposed that ethics is a central concept to leadership. Furthermore, literature has suggested that the philosophical underpinnings of effective leadership connect ethical and moral decision making with leader behavior (Crowther, 2012b; Henson, 2015).

Ethical and Moral Leadership

Although much has been written regarding the *what* and *how* of ethical and moral leadership, current research is now focusing on the *why* of ethical and moral leadership (V. L. Allen, 2006; Crowther, 2012a; Henson, 2015). *Ethical leadership* flows from the foundational principles of "respect, service, justice, honesty, and community" (Northouse, 2015, p. 341). Ethical leadership is an *others-focused* construct wherein the leader demonstrates the aforementioned principles for the betterment of the follower or organization. Northouse (2015) suggested that toxic and unethical leadership is nothing more than a perversion of ethical leadership. Likewise, Bandura (1999) stated that in order for individuals/leaders to behave in an unethical or immoral manner, they must first morally disengage by justifying their behavior, minimizing the consequences of unethical action, or dehumanizing the victims of their immoral and unethical decision making.

Moral leadership and ethical leadership, though similar, are not synonymous. Within ethical leadership, there is an understanding of morality. Although some equate *morality* with *ethics*, Rae (2009) stated that morality refers to "moral knowledge" (p. 15) and ethics refers to "moral reasoning" (p. 15). Some have defined *ethics* as the systematic exploration of right and wrong, while others have suggested that *morals* refer to the standards that define what is right and what is wrong (Johnson, 2013; Rae, 2009; Rhode, 2006).

The etymological roots of the term *ethics* are connected to the Greek concepts of character and custom, while the etymological roots of the term *moral* are connected to the concepts of habitual character (Rhode, 2006). Simply put: morality, *right belief*, influences ethics, *right action* (Johnson, 2013; Rae, 2009; Rhode, 2006). Since the literature has implied that *others-focused behavior* is central to the ethical leadership framework, one could argue that the ethical leadership found within servant leadership, authentic leadership, transformational leadership, and spiritual leadership constitutes a virtue-based deontological system whereby moral knowledge influences moral reasoning, which ultimately produces ethical behavior (Avolio & Gardner, 2005; Bass, 2009; Burns, 1978; Patterson, 2003; Rae, 2009). Research has posed that certain forms of utilitarianism, ethical egoism, and relativism negatively elevate self-interest in a way that violates the ethical foundations of the aforementioned values-based leadership theories (V. L. Allen, 2006; Becker, 2009; Rae, 2009; Schuh, Zhang, & Tian, 2013). Yet, Ciulla (1995, 2005) claimed that pure altruism is an extreme manifestation within leadership behavior since it is natural for one to consider one's own interests. However, what is not revealed in the current literature is how the act of leading may influence or shape the self-interests of a leader.

Ethical leadership is a modern construct with ancient roots that connects to multiple contemporary leadership theories. The word *ethics* and the development of ethical theory trace back to Platonic and Aristotelian philosophy (Northouse, 2015). Ethics involves the motives, virtues, and principles that determine *right* and *wrong* human behavior (Northouse, 2015). However, since ethical behavior flows from ethical character, one cannot fully explore *leadership ethics* without also exploring the moral underpinnings of ethics. Northouse (2015) proposed two domains for the theoretical study of ethics: *conduct* and *character*. Teleological theories such as ethical egoism and utilitarianism focus on the consequences of a leader's conduct, while virtue-based leadership theories such as servant leadership and transformational leadership focus on a leader's character (Northouse, 2015). Ethical egoism suggests that a person should only act for the greater good of self, whereas utilitarianism suggests that a person should behave in a manner that benefits the greater good of the "greatest number" (Northouse, 2015, p. 314). The opposite of ethical egoism is altruism, which suggests "actions are moral if their primary purpose is to promote the best interests of others" (Northouse, 2015, p. 335). Altruism is a central component of both servant leadership theory and transformational leadership theory (Northouse, 2015; Patterson, 2003).

For example, Patterson (2003) developed a virtue-based model for servant leadership that includes seven constructs: (a) agapao love, (b) humility, (c), altruism, (d) vision, (e) trust, (f) empowerment, and (g) service. According to Patterson's model of servant leadership theory, altruism refers to the selfless, humble, and respectful consideration of others. In fact, Patterson argued that a "servant leader does good acts with the right motive" (p. 8). While teleological theories seek to explain how certain actions produce certain outcomes, deontological theories seek to explain how some actions are inherently good regardless of the consequences (Northouse, 2015). Given this, the present study suggests that the unethical behaviors of some leaders are the result of a form of ethical egoism that is often mistaken for altruism.

Brown, Treviño, et al. (2005) stated that ethical leadership relates in some way to "consideration behavior, honesty, trust in the leader, interactional fairness" (p. 117) and the idealized influence dimension of transformational leadership displayed in socialized charismatic leadership. Because followers often look to leaders for guidance, it is assumed that a leader's ethical behavior has a direct impact on the ethical behavior of followers (Brown, Treviño, et al., 2005). Thus, Brown, Treviño, et al. defined ethical leadership as "the demonstration of normatively appropriate conduct through personal actions and interpersonal relationships, and the promotion of such conduct to followers through two-way communication, reinforcement, and decision-making" (p. 117). Furthermore, in order for an ethical leader to influence follower ethics, the leader must be perceived as an attractive and credible role model (Brown, Treviño, et al., 2005).

Brown and Treviño (2014) sought to test the theories regarding the centrality of ethics in leadership and role modeling by conducting a field study that examined the relationship between three types of ethical role models and ethical leadership. They revealed that having childhood ethical role models and career-level ethical role models both positively affect the development of ethical leadership in followers. I believe that the current pervasiveness of ethical leadership failure is the result of distorted role modeling and idealized influence.

According to Yukl (2013), leadership is synonymous with influence, which includes the various ways by which a leader shapes the ethical behaviors of followers. In order to judge the ethical behavior of a leader, one must consider the purpose of the behavior, the correlation between the behavior and moral standards, and the effects of the behavior on the leader and others (Yukl, 2013). However, behaviors that present as morally acceptable are sometimes used for unethical purposes (Yukl, 2013). Although moral and ethical standards vary across different cultures, research has suggested that the exploitation of others is considered immoral and unethical regardless of culture (Yukl, 2013). For example, "to use kindness to gain the trust of people who will later be exploited" (Yukl, 2013, p. 342) is considered universally unethical. Given this, I believe that unethical decision making is linked to self-serving exploitation.

According to Burns (1978), leadership is not just a matter of holding power or exerting force but rather a relationship that manifests along two types: transactional leadership or transforming leadership. Transactional leaders view leading as a means for exchanging *one thing for another*, whereas transformational leaders view leading as a means for empowering and inspiring followers (Burns, 1978, 2003). Burns (1978) stated, "Power and leadership are measured by the degree of production of intended effects" (p. 21). Tensions arise in leadership when ethics are divorced from morals and values for the sake of the perceived greater good (Burns, 1978). Thus, although a leader may fit within the transactional framework apart from ethics, they are not truly transformational without the guidance of morally based ethical values such as empowerment, justice, and equality (Burns, 2003). If Burns' *ethical bridge* between transactional and transformational leadership is true, then this book fills the gap in the literature by exploring how variables such as stress and trauma undercut the ethical dimensions of leadership.

Avolio (2010) argued that although leadership involves personality, context, and influence, it is also *system* comprised of *inputs, processes,* and *outcomes.* Thus, the development of future leaders hinges on the optimization of the *system,* which must be examined over a period of time (Avolio, 2010). Avolio referred to this construct as *full-range leadership development.* One factor in effective leadership development is the concept of "moral perspective" (Avolio, 2010, p. 210), which determines how individuals allow their "guiding internal beliefs and values to drive their actions" (p. 210). Given this, I believe that the presence of stress in the life of a leader interacts with *moral perspective,* which may subsequently compromise the leadership *system.*

According to Brown and Mitchell (2010), "Leaders set the tone for organizational goals and behavior" (p. 583). This includes functioning as a *moral manager* who uses the position and resources of leadership to promote ethical leadership amongst the organization (Brown & Mitchell, 2010). It is important to note that this construct extends to both the leader's' personal and professional life (Brown & Mitchell, 2010). Furthermore, Brown and Mitchell argued that in order for effective moral management and ethical modeling to take place, "role models must be credible in terms of moral behavior" (p. 585). Brown and Mitchell suggested that future research into ethical and unethical leadership consider the emerging trend of *emotion* as it relates to leadership.

Brown and Treviño (2006) conducted a literature review on the construct of ethical leadership as it relates to the moral dimensions of spiritual leadership, authentic leadership, and transformational leadership. They suggested that ethical leadership is similar to the moral dimensions of the aforementioned leadership theories in that they all involve (a) altruism, (b), integrity, and (c) role modeling. However, ethical leaders emphasize moral management, whereas as transformational leaders emphasize "vision, values, and intellectual stimulation" (Brown & Treviño, 2006, p. 598), authentic leaders emphasize "authenticity and self-awareness" (p. 598); and spiritual leaders emphasize hope, faith, vision, and "work as vocation" (p. 598). Brown and Treviño suggested that future research explore the differences between ethical and unethical leadership in order to aid in effective leadership development. Therefore, as this book moves forward we will examine how the emotions associated with leadership fatigue affect the credibility of moral management and how moral management separates ethical from unethical leadership. Since leadership is synonymous with influence (Yukl, 2013), and since ethics is central to leadership (Burns, 2003; Northouse, 2015), and since leaders serve as moral role models for followers (Brown & Treviño, 2014), it is important to explore how the moral component of ethical leadership impacts the ethical decision-making process.

Moral Component of Ethical Leadership

Rae (2009) suggested that moral questions are the bedrock of the most vital issues of humanity. In the Old Testament, the concept of ethics centered on the Hebrew word *qadosh* or "holy" (Rae, 2009, p. 32). This term implies a form of *setting apart* that involves adherence to the commands of God. Within these commands exists a link between personal and social ethics (Rae, 2009). For example, in the Book of Leviticus, one finds laws about personal worship and real estate placed in a singular volume. Rae argued that although New Testament ethics emphasize ecclesial morality more than institutional morality, the ethics of love, peace, virtue, and joy all connect with the idea of being set apart for Christ-likeness in all situations. Furthermore, Rae argued that it is appropriate to treat the terms *ethics* and *morals* as separate constructs since morality deals with the content of *right* and *wrong* and ethics deals with the processes of determining *right* and *wrong*. This text places morality within the larger framework of ethics, with the Hebrew and Christian Scriptures serving as the source of all that is truly moral.

Unlike Rae (2009), Kanungo and Mendonca (1996) suggested that morals and ethics are interchangeable terms since "what is ethical is moral, and what is unethical is immoral" (p. 33). In their research on the ethical dimensions of leadership, Kanungo and Mendonca contended that morality cannot be limited to that which is legal or illegal or to moral law at the expense of motive, situation, and social consequences. However, they also suggested that a total focus on *motive* leads to moral subjectivism, while a total focus on *situation* leads to situational ethics; both leave room for unethical and immoral behavior. Therefore, one way to resolve this tension is to look at four factors that influence ethical decision making and behavior: the act, the motive, the situation, and the impact of stress and trauma on the leader's decision-making processes.

Ethical Decision Making and Leadership Theories

De Cremer et al. (2010) argued that to "increase moral awareness and manage mistrust" (p. 1), scholars must "zoom in" (p. 1) on why ethical failures occur. They believed that the answer for ethical failure is found within the field of psychology. Specifically, instead of trying to prevent ethical failures, De Cremer et al. suggested that policy makers and organizational leaders should gain a deeper understanding of behavioral ethics, which includes developing trust by rapidly responding to unethical behavior in order to reduce the prevalence of ethical failure. Given this, the current study does not seek to eliminate ethical failures but instead seeks to build on the work of De Cremer et al. by providing an answer for *why* ethical failures occur. I am convinced that leadership fatigue (i.e., trauma and stress) is a cause of ethical failure.

Schaubroek et al. (2002) examined how ethical leadership embeds across various organizational levels. They examined a sample of deployed soldiers in the U.S. army with results indicating that ethical leadership *diffuses* throughout an organization as opposed to just *trickling* down from senior leaders to subordinates. According to Schaubroek et al., "Ethical leadership at higher levels promotes ethical culture at those levels, which in turn facilitates a more favorable impact of ethical leadership on ethical culture at the next lower level" (p. 1073). Furthermore, senior leaders, direct supervisors, and the ethical culture of an organization all play a role in shaping subordinate ethical behavior (Schaubroek et al., 2002). If ethical leadership diffuses through various organizational levels with positive results, it is possible that unethical behavior also diffuses through an organization in the same manner with negative results. The Schaubroek et al. study is relevant to the current study in that they both involve the military context in combat environments. Given this, I believe that the life of King David will demonstrate that the converse of the Schaubroek et al. study is also true.

Kouzes and Posner (2006) stated that exemplary leaders model the way for followers by clarifying values, which includes the promotion of ethical behavior. According to their model of exemplary leadership, it is the responsibility of leadership to fully comprehend "the values, standards, ethics, and ideals" (p. 41) that not only guide their decisions but also influence the decision making of subordinates. This is critical since followers look to leaders for guidance, especially in competitive, stressful, traumatic, or other crisis situations (Kouzes & Posner, 2006). Therefore, the use of the narrative in 2 Samuel 11:1-27 should demonstrate how King David modeled an *unethical way* that negatively influenced his follower's decision making.

According to Hoyt and Price (2015), the role and act of leading often leads to a form of moral permissibility wherein leaders may engage in unethical behavior to achieve certain leadership goals. This argument is connected to the social role theory of unethical behavior and demonstrates how "self-construal influences group-based ethical decision making" (Hoyt & Price, 2015, p. 531). Self-construal refers to how one perceives one's actions and position within a larger group relationship (Hoyt & Price, 2015). This book, along with much of the research on ethical leadership, focuses on the self-serving nature of unethical decision making (Hoyt & Price, 2015; Midgen, 2015).

For example, Midgen (2015) conducted a study on unethical behavior in educational psychology services. Midgen revealed, "The context and vulnerable position of some educational psychology services poses risks for ethical (including financial) misconduct" (p. 92). This misconduct often stems from good intentions that fail to consider various ethical dilemmas that arise as the leader shifts his or her focus from the greater good toward self. This book builds on the existing literature by exploring unethical decision making from the perspective of self-service as well as the perspective of moral permissibility brought about by a leader assuming that his or her decisions benefit the greater good.

Bass (2009) stated that even the most successful leaders may eventually succumb to unethical behavior. This unethical behavior usually stems from a leader's misguided belief in his or her ability to control the outcome of certain situations (Bass, 2009). Bass surveyed 100 members of the executive panel of the Academy of Management. Of those surveyed, "87% said it was a common rationale to 'bend the rules' to get the job done, and 77% said this was a common justification if performance standards were unfair and overly restrictive" (Bass, 2009, p. 210). Furthermore, Bass argued that it is the primary duty of ethical leaders to truthfully pursue fairness while avoiding the harm of others. However, the complex nature of executive leadership often makes it difficult for one to live out the aforementioned ethical imperatives. Nevertheless, moral reasoning, which is inherent in ethical leadership, allows one to ask "what is the right thing to do" (Bass, 2009, p. 215) while also considering how the "right thing" (p. 215) affects others. If Bass' concepts regarding the eventuality of unethical leadership and the role of moral reasoning are correct, then this book will build on the current literature by demonstrating how leadership fatigue accelerates unethical behavior while also clouding moral reasoning.

Ethical leadership is connected to several leadership theories. In the same way that ethical leadership further develops transactional leadership and transformational leadership, it also plays a critical role in authentic leadership theory and spiritual leadership theory. Avolio and Gardner (2005) suggested that positive ethical climates directly impact the development of authentic leadership. Fry (2003) stated that spiritual leadership depends on a leader's ability to "get in touch with their core values and communicate them to followers through vision and personal actions" (p. 710). Although authentic leadership theory originates from humanistic and *self-oriented* constructs, the authentic leader is ethically *self-aware* and *self-regulatory* (Avolio & Gardner, 2005). According to Avolio and Gardner, "Self-regulation is the process through which authentic leaders align their values with their intentions and actions" (p. 325). Furthermore, Bass (2009) stated, "Authentic transformational leaders align their interests with the interests of others and may sacrifice their own interests for the common good" (p. 224). If this is true regarding authentic, transformational, and spiritual leadership, then this book will demonstrate how leadership fatigue impacts the common morals-based thread between various leadership theories.

According to Ciulla (1995), the first 70 years of leadership research failed to adequately address the *sense* of good associated with moral leadership. This is partly due to the *emotional and normative baggage* associated with the word *leader* (Ciulla, 1995). However, the last 20 years of research, while critical of ethical failure in leadership, has addressed the gap regarding the *sense* of good by not only focusing on what a leader does but on what a leader should *do* and *be* (Ciulla, 2005). Ciulla (1995) claimed that in spite of the overwhelming evidence on the pervasiveness of unethical leadership, few researchers have dedicated their studies toward the prevention of unethical leadership through ethical leadership development. I address the gap presented by Ciulla by exploring the *sense* of good associated with ethical leadership and by exploring how leadership fatigue impacts what a leader should *do* and *be*.

Crowther (2012a) suggested that a "focus on ethics and integrity is important in the contemporary context of leadership issues" (p. 45) due to an increase in scandal and unethical decision making at various levels within the organizational leadership framework. Crowther used the Christian Scriptures to explore authentic and kenotic leadership. Crowther suggested that authentic leadership as seen in 1 Peter involves a leader shifting his or her perspective from *self* toward *others* through a kenotic embracing of suffering for the sake of God and others. Furthermore, Crowther argued that the changed perspective found within 1 Peter's authentic and kenotic leadership involves a change in ethic. Both authentic and kenotic leadership involve one placing the needs and well-being of others above one's own agenda through ethical moral development (Crowther, 2012a). I build on Crowther's work by using the Hebrew Scriptures to inductively explore the ethical motives of leadership within high-stress contexts.

Henson (2015) further developed Crowther's theories on authentic leadership by applying a similar methodology to Titus in order to examine the ethical development of leaders with a special emphasis on moral development. According to Henson, moral development is "(a) transgenerational, (b) relational, (c) spiritual, (d) cognitive, (e) behavioral, and (f) experiential" (p. 160). Henson revealed a direct link between "inner transformation and ethical conduct" (p. 166). Thus, inner transformation should cause a leader to pursue more than just the societal minimum when it comes to ethical behavior (Henson, 2015). Henson also suggested that moral development produces ethical behavior, especially in chaotic times. Given this, it should be found that leadership fatigue impacted the moral dimension of ethical decision making in King David as seen in 2 Samuel 11:1-27.

Several values-based leadership theories link to ethical and moral leadership. Most of the research on these theories has explored the traits, behaviors, and dyadic relationships associated with the constructs of the theories. However, there is room within the literature to explore variables that may interfere with the effective and ethical application of values-based leadership theories. This is especially true when it comes to the role of leadership fatigue. Thus, in order to analyze the impact of leadership fatigue on ethical and moral decision making, we must first understand the gap in the literature regarding ethical leadership and stress.

Ethical Leadership and Stress

V. L. Allen (2006) sought to counter a perceived overemphasis on effective leadership by exploring moral failure in exceptional leaders. V. L. Allen employed a content analysis of critical statements made by two high-level leaders. V. L. Allen revealed that both of the failed leaders used dehumanizing language, self-exoneration, blame shifting, and a form of moral reasoning to justify their perceived failures. According to V. L. Allen, both of the leaders who experienced moral failure had "publicly endorsed a strong and lifelong devotion to their faith and to the application of faith-based behavior within their leadership roles such as the use of prayer on behalf of followers, the organization, or its constituency" (p. 210). Furthermore, both of the failed leaders had written extensively on the subject of organizational ethics. In spite of an apparent foundation in ethics, morality, and spirituality, both failed leaders blamed fatigue, physical needs, poor judgement, and sacrificial action "being done in the greater interest of the organization" (V. L..Allen, 2006, p. 211) for their failures. V. L. Allen suggested that the stress of leadership serves as one of the key variables associated with moral failure and unethical leadership. This book builds on V. L. Allen's work by arguing that stress, when left unchecked and coupled with trauma, facilitates unethical decision making because the *role* and *act* of leading is inherently stressful and potentially traumatic.

According to Crowther (2012b), leaders are frequently tested through suffering, pressure, and the paradoxical power dynamic of selfless leadership. Thus, stress is not an excuse for failure but rather a mechanism for the development of resilience and positive ethical change (Crowther, 2012b). Crowther also stated that a leader should use "power and authority properly since they are moderated by the internal issues of good character" ("The Big Picture," para. 6). In Crowther's paradigm, *good character* is developed through *testing*, which brings strength and joy in times of stress and pressure. However, without a vision for the future, leaders may not redeem stress as found within Crowther's framework. Therefore, this book explores how leadership fatigue and trauma cloud a leader's vision for a morally positive future, which subsequently results in unethical behavior.

Bandura (1999) suggested that there are several mechanisms for moral disengagement. According to Bandura, moral disengagement involves (a) moral justification, (b) palliative comparison, (c) euphemistic labeling, (d) minimizing or misconstruing consequences, (e) dehumanization, (f) attribution of blame, and (g) the displacement or diffusion of responsibility. Furthermore, Bandura's theories find confirmation in the work of Crowther (2012b) and V. L. Allen (2006) in that all three studies confirmed the gradualist nature of unethical behavior. Given this, in later chapters I will demonstrate how 2 Samuel 11:1-27 is an exemplar for moral disengagement with an emphasis on how trauma and stress interact with the mechanisms of moral disengagement.

According to Rhode (2006), the substance of effective leadership is morally infused ethical leadership. Rhode claimed that there would be no scientific inquiry into moral and ethical failure if it were not for a "succession of scandals" (p. 1) at the highest levels of leadership. Moreover, 60 years of leadership failure has not produced a substantial scholarly response to the prevalence of unethical and immoral leadership (Rhode, 2006). Rhode argued that research on moral and ethical leadership should focus on "leadership in business contexts because this is where most work had been done and where the need in practice appears greatest" (p. 3). What was not fully explored in Rhode's work is *why* the need is great in business contexts. Thus, this book fills the gaps identified by Rhode by presenting leadership fatigue as a potential source for the preponderance of leadership failure in business contexts.

In environments of constant change and uncertainty, leaders and followers need a set of waypoints that allow for one to remain consistent in their integrity (Tichy & McGill, 2003). Tichy and McGill (2003) argued that ethics and values "serve as fixed-points" ("People Change Rules," para. 3) that not only aid in determining right from wrong, they also aid in the total health of the individual. According to Tichy and McGill, an overemphasis on unethical behavior (what not to do) has left a gap in the literature regarding virtuous honoring (what one *should* do). Moreover, by focusing on the "absence of harm" (Tichy & McGill, 2003, "En Route to Virtuousness," para. 5) many forsake opportunities to create *good* for the sake of honoring others. Thus, the pressure to perform and produce without the presence of virtuousness may cause individuals to experience a pressure toward unethical behavior (Tichy & McGill, 2003). Given this, the study presented in this book seeks to expand the work of Tichy and McGill by demonstrating how leadership fatigue undermines the role of virtuousness in ethical leadership.

The *act* of leading not only involves the responsibilities and tasks associated with the *role* of leadership, it also involves one balancing the ethical weight of "power, prestige, information, consistency, and loyalty" with "sound moral reasoning" (Johnson, 2013, p. 7). Johnson argued that failing to balance the aforementioned leads some leaders toward the *dark side* of leadership. Thus, toxic leaders typically exploit power, information, responsibility, and the well-being of others to further their own agenda. According to Johnson, the dark side of leadership involves six *shadows* that foster toxic leadership: (a) the shadow of power, (b) the shadow of privilege, (c) the shadow of mismanaged information, (d) the shadow of inconsistency, (e) the shadow of misplaced and broken loyalties, and (f) the shadow of irresponsibility. Johnson claimed that refusing to acknowledge the impact of coercive, reward, legitimate, expert, or referent power on the ethical decision-making process leaves leaders exposed to the trappings of the dark side of leadership. Furthermore, Johnson noted that the contextual pressure to maintain or achieve certain numbers, conform to group expectations, or appease dissenters may cause a leader to "cast a shadow" (p. 60). I build on Johnson's dark side construct by demonstrating how the pressure of leadership manifested as leadership fatigue serves as an antecedent to the six shadows of unethical leadership outlined by Johnson.

Becker (2009) suggested that leadership should be based on both moral principles and ethical vision. However, since the cultural construct of leadership often lends itself to hierarchical models, and since "business leadership is characterized by asymmetrical power-authority relationships in hierarchical organizations" (Becker, 2009, p. 8), what leadership *should* be and what leadership actually *becomes* in the corporate context are often miles apart. Thus, leaders are often under pressure to perform to maintain their positions at the *top* both organizationally and culturally. Becker contended that laws are not enough to counter the pressure of executive level leadership. Rather, if an organization wants to achieve true success and excellence, then moral codes must be instituted, practiced, and enforced across all levels of the organization as a way of countering the pressure one faces to use unethical means to accomplish organizational goals (Becker, 2009). This book not only seeks to demonstrate how moral codes are compromised by extreme trauma and pressure, but it also builds on Becker's theories by demonstrating the susceptibility to unethical decision making that exists in asymmetrical power-authority relationships.

Schuh et al. (2013) also presented power asymmetry as the converse of moral leadership, which has implications for ethical decision making. According to Schuh et al., transformational leadership is often presented as a positive amongst values-based leadership theories. However, Schuh et al. suggested that although transformational leadership behavior enhances the positive effects of altruism on in-role and extra-role behavior, it also enhances "the adverse consequences of self-centered (i.e., authoritarian) leadership behavior with regards to followers' reactions" (p. 636). Schuh et al. suggested that future studies on transformational leadership should explore the moral and authoritarian aspects of effective leadership. Since it is proven that ethical leadership connects to transformational leadership and authoritarian leadership, I will address the authoritarian issues found in the Schuh et al. study by presenting leadership fatigue as a mediating factor between effective leadership and dark-side leadership.

Leadership involves various expectations and internal and external pressures. The goal of the current study is to identify how those pressures, defined as leadership fatigue, impact ethical and moral leadership on various levels, including the decision-making process. Based on the evidence, ethical leadership not only connects to several values-based leadership theories, it also informs the decision-making process. Furthermore, ethics is a proven and central construct within the discipline of leadership. Since virtually every leadership theory involves a moral and ethical element, it is important to explore both *why* and *how* ethical failure happens.

The world needs ethical and moral leaders, and the literature has supported the efficacy of ethical and moral leadership. However, leaders in a variety of organizational contexts consistently fail morally and ethically, and the literature has not adequately addressed multiple variables that may be the underlying cause of ethical and moral failure. In particular, the research has indicated that high-profile leaders are more susceptible to ethical and moral leadership failures than other leaders (Johnson, 2013; Rhode, 2006; Tichy & McGill, 2003). However, the literature has not explored how being high profile may contribute to PTS or leadership fatigue. In spite of volumes of research on ethical and moral leadership, decision-making processes, and training advancements designed to stop leadership failure, organizations still struggle to prevent unethical decision making and behavior (De Cremer et al., 2010; Midgen, 2015). Furthermore, a significant gap exists in the literature regarding the concept of leadership fatigue and its effect on ethical and moral decision making.

At the center of this problem is the definition of what it means to lead. Yukl (2013) defined leadership as "the process of influencing others to understand and agree about what needs to be done and how to do it, and the process of facilitating individual and collective efforts to accomplish shared objectives" (p.7). Leadership definitions include elements of trait-based theories that focus on leader charisma and follower-based theories that focus on dyadic relationships (Bass, 2009; Northouse, 2015; Yukl, 2013). Although leadership is defined and developed across a broad spectrum, one cannot fully explore leadership in a fixed place (Avolio, 2010). Avolio (2010) argued that since it takes years for one to develop a moral and ethical base, the exploration of leadership development should take place over a period of time. In spite of the aforementioned definitions of leadership, none of these theories explores the assumption that, by nature, leadership is tiresome and potentially traumatic to the leader. Although the current literature explores the impact of secondary trauma, job satisfaction, and pretrauma on workplace stress and PTS, there is a need to explore how the very act of leading impacts the moral and ethical processes of the leader as well as why a leader may respond to trauma with immoral and unethical decision making and behavior (DiGangi et al., 2013; Hendron et al., 2012, 2014). Thus, more significant research is needed to explore the impact of leadership fatigue on moral and ethical decision making and behavior.

Along with the gap in the literature relating to leadership fatigue, there is also a need for varied methodologies in the exploration of ethical and moral leadership as they relate to trauma and stress. Since values-based ethics is often connected with sacred texts, it is necessary to explore ethical and moral behavior through the lens of theology (Rae, 2009). As the queen of the sciences, theology as explored through exegetical methodologies provides researchers with a process for "thinking about life" (Stone & Duke, 2013, p. 3) in a way that differs from traditional quantitative methodologies.

Moreover, qualitative methodologies such as hermeneutical phenomenology and sociorhetorical analysis lend themselves to the exploration of essences and meaning in a way that considers the various layers of one's personal experience, whereas quantitative methodologies function within the strict and objective confines of prescribed instrumentation (Patton, 2002; Robbins, 1996a).

Because character, morality, ethics, spirituality, and ontology address the inner issues of leadership, it is important to utilize data and methodologies that also focus on issues of personhood and being (Crowther, 2012b). In fact, several recent leadership studies have utilized the Hebrew and Christian Scriptures as the data source for sociorhetorical exploration into authentic leadership, transformational leadership, servant leadership, follower development, and ethical leadership (Crowther, 2012a; Henson, 2015; Huizing, 2013; Perry, 2016). Furthermore, much has been written about what a leader should do, while in-depth studies into how and why leaders behave ethically and morally are limited at best (Brown & Treviño, 2006). Brown and Treviño (2006) proposed that a high level of moral reasoning "positively relates to ethical leadership . . . [and] internal locus of control is positively related to ethical leadership" (p. 605). Therefore, it is important to explore these propositions along with the aforementioned literature gap by using the Hebrew and Christian Scriptures as the main source of data.

The primary problem addressed by this study is the epidemic of moral and ethical failure amongst executive level leaders. A deeper understanding of why leaders may make unethical and immoral decisions could enhance leadership development processes in a way that reverses the trend of rapid ethical and moral failure. These results could benefit both secular and Christian organizational leadership paradigms. Therefore, by the end of this book we will have explored the constructs of trauma, trauma-related stress, and burnout as they relate to ethical and moral failure.

CHAPTER 2

War is Traumatic and So is Leadership

The world needs ethical and moral leaders, and past research has supported the efficacy of ethical and moral leadership. However, leaders in a variety of organizational contexts consistently fail morally and ethically, and the literature has not adequately addressed multiple variables that may be the underlying cause of ethical and moral failure. In particular, past research has indicated that high-profile leaders are more susceptible to ethical and moral leadership failures than other leaders (Johnson, 2013; Rhode, 2006; Tichy & McGill, 2003). However, the literature has not explored *how* being high profile may contribute to PTS or leadership fatigue. In spite of volumes of research on ethical and moral leadership, decision-making processes, and training advancements designed to stop leadership failure, organizations still struggle to prevent unethical decision making and behavior (De Cremer et al., 2010; Midgen, 2015). Furthermore, a significant gap exists in the research regarding the concept of *leadership fatigue* and its effect on ethical and moral decision making.

Maslach, Schaufeli, and Leiter (2001) argued that burnout and workplace stress are characterized by both dehumanization and a form of emotional instability and exhaustion that leads to negative performance outputs. Research also has suggested that burnout directly impacts one's cognitive function (Diestel, Cosmar, & Schmidt, 2013). Stress-related burnout is also prevalent in others-focused industries such as social work, psychology, and pastoral ministry (Diaconescu, 2015; Hendron, Irving, & Taylor, 2012, 2014). *Compassion fatigue* and *burnout syndrome* are related in that they both stem from a prolonged care for the needs of others (Diaconescu, 2015).

However, they differ in that the latter is often connected with a lack of professional satisfaction, while the former is associated with the "cost of caring" (Diaconescu, 2015, p. 60).

For example, researchers have suggested that professional clergy, although initially enthusiastic and motivated in their work, often succumb to compassion fatigue and burnout due to stress-related vocational dissatisfaction (Grosch & Olsen, 2000). In fact, in research on clergy burnout, Forward (2000) suggested that the pastoral–congregational framework, the CEO/Shepherd metaphor, and pressures from the church growth literature compound what is an inherently stressful vocation. This compounded pressure may lead to immoral and unethical behavior as the leader attempts to cope with the stresses of the vocation (Hendron et al., 2012, 2014).

Although trauma is often associated with combat, assault, or the threat of physical harm, Tanner, Wherry, and Zvonkovic (2013) suggested that dramatic shifts in *life* also produce trauma. Despite individuals' ability to redeem traumatic experiences for positive outcomes, in many cases it is difficult for them to discuss their trauma for the sake of research (Jaffe, DiLillo, Hoffman, Haikalis, & Dykstra, 2015; Williams & Allen, 2015). Furthermore, studies have suggested a connection between posttraumatic stress (PTS), anxiety, marked behavioral changes, restlessness, and a disinterest in previous activities (Contractor, Elhai, Ractliffe, & Forbes, 2013; Koffel, Polusny, Arbisi, & Erbes, 2012). Zheng et al. (2015) argued that in morally intense situations such as combat, a lack of ethical leadership compounds these morally intense situations in a way that increases emotional exhaustion in followers. In the United States, the last 15 years of continual combat warfare has produced a wealth of information on PTS, traumatic brain injury, the impact of moral disengagement on the psychosocial realities of soldiers, military leaders, and military families; appropriate PTS screening methods; the role of stigma and shame in PTS reporting; and other non-military vocations that are at risk for PTS (Blais & Renshaw, 2013; Chamberlin, 2012; Conybeare, Behar, Solomon, Newman, & Borkovec, 2012; Grossman, 2009; Harman & Lee, 2010; Koffel et al., 2012; Reger et al., 2013; Skogstad et al., 2013; Sundin, Fear, Iversen, Rona, & Wessely, 2010). However, no much research exists regarding the relationship between PTS and ethical and moral leadership.

Leadership Fatigue

I define leadership fatigue as a synthesis of various trauma, job-related stress, and morally intense situations and their impact on the processes of ethical and moral leadership. Zheng et al. (2015) touched on elements of leadership fatigue in their study of emotional exhaustion and morally intense situations. According to Zheng et al., ethical leadership is salient in "situations where decisions frequently affect life and death (e.g., military operations, fire-fighting, law enforcement, and health care)" (p. 732) or in situations where "the magnitude of consequences is high" (p. 732). Zheng et al. surveyed 258 service members deployed in a combat zone; they found that low levels of ethical leadership contribute to emotional exhaustion in followers. Furthermore, they provided a link between morally intense situations and ethical leadership. However, they did not differentiate between emotional exhaustion as an individual occurrence or a team-based phenomenon. Likewise, they did not address variables such as trauma and job-related stress. Given this, I move beyond isolating emotional exhaustion or morally intense environments as mediators for ethical leadership by combining several stress-related terms into one singular concept: leadership fatigue.

Stress and Burnout

According to Maslach et al. (2001), job burnout is a "psychological syndrome" (p. 399) that stems from "chronic interpersonal stress" (p. 399). Maslach et al. suggested that burnout is characterized by three dimensions: exhaustion, cynicism, and inefficacy. The various stages of research into job burnout show a consistent link between the presence of stress and the behaviors associated with job burnout. During the *pioneer phase* of job burnout research, concepts such as emotional depletion and loss of motivation were linked to care-giving professions (Maslach et al., 2001). During the *empirical phase* of job burnout research, instruments such as the Maslach Burnout Inventory connected job burnout to job satisfaction, turnover, and organizational commitment (Maslach et al., 2001). Additionally, Maslach et al. claimed that the "relational transactions" (p. 400) inherent in service-oriented professions are found to lead to emotional detachment and cynicism, which subsequently results in dehumanization in the caregiver/

client relationship. Because the current study proposes that the presence of stress is a key contributing factor toward unethical leadership, this book builds on the work of Maslach et al. by exploring the link between leadership fatigue, stress-induced job burnout, and ethical leadership.

Diestel et al. (2013) also connected job burnout with stress. They suggested that burnout is not only linked to multiple job stressors, it also negatively impacts cognitive (executive) control when high exhaustion is present in employees. Cognitive control refers to the interrelation of task shifting, information processing, and response inhibition as they relate to achieving job-related goals (Diestel et al., 2013). According to Diestel et al., "Reduced executive control impairs successful adaption to job demands" (p. 177). Thus, job performance is impaired as one experiences an increase in high levels of exhaustion and high levels of demand on their cognitive control (Diestel et al., 2013). Given this, I believe that unethical leadership is also a result compromised of cognitive control and stress-related job burnout.

Compassion fatigue is a term that scholars have related to stress-induced job burnout amongst care givers (Diaconescu, 2015). Compassion fatigue is closely related to burnout syndrome (Diaconescu, 2015). Although many health care professionals, social workers, and educational workers are initially enthusiastic about their vocation, the constant presence of distress, eustress, or traumatic stress often leads to secondary trauma (Diaconescu, 2015). According to Diaconescu (2015), "The ones who suffer from compassion fatigue start seeing deeply negative changes in their personal and professional lives" (p. 57), and those who experience burnout deal with "chronic physical and emotional fatigue, the depletion of the empathic resources and of compassion, boredom, cynicism, diminution of enthusiasm, temporary distress, and depression symptoms" (p. 60). Furthermore, secondary trauma is almost identical to symptoms such as "hyper-excitability, de-personalization, de-realization, and dissociative amnesia" (Diaconescu, 2015, p. 60), which are associated with posttraumatic stress disorder (PTSD). I seek to add to Diaconescu's work by demonstrating how compassion fatigue, burnout, and secondary trauma-related stress impact the ethical decision-making process.

Hendron et al. (2012) suggested that clergy are especially susceptible to secondary trauma, burnout, and compassion fatigue. Clergy stress scores were similar to the stress scores of counselors and health care providers based on the Traumatic Stress Institute Belief Scale (Hendron et al., 2012). Likewise, a majority of clergy tested with the Maslach Burnout Inventory showed moderate to high emotional exhaustion (Hendron et al., 2012). One cause of stress and burnout in clergy is their exposure to "traumatic material" (Hendron et al., 2012, p. 223).

In a follow-up study, Hendron et al. (2014) discovered that clergy are typically unaware of their risk for secondary trauma. Hendron et al. revealed that clergy who were exposed to trauma or who were suffering from secondary trauma experienced both cognitive and emotional disruptions. Moreover, some of the clergy surveyed made little or no mention of God or faith when discussing their experiences with trauma or the stress of ministry, which could indicate a weakening of spiritualty's role in safeguarding leader's from the impact of stress (Hendron et al., 2014). Since there is a connection between ethical leadership and spirituality, and since clergy are susceptible to burnout and compassion fatigue, and since little is known about the cost of stress and compassion fatigue amongst spiritual leaders, this book closes the apparent gap by demonstrating how leadership fatigue impacts ethical and moral leadership.

According to Grosch and Olsen (2000), clergy experience burnout because of external stress such as demanding bureaucratic systems, a lack of professional support, and various difficulties associated with church life. Likewise, clergy also experience internal stress that often flows from "high idealism, Type-A personalities, narcissism, and perfectionism" (Grosch & Olsen, 2000, p. 619). Grosch and Olsen believed that *take a day off* is inadequate advice given the guilt that is often associated with *rest* amongst clergy. Furthermore, clergy are susceptible to the *God complex* or the feeling that it is on their shoulders to fix everyone's problems while also serving as a representative of God to the congregation (Grosch & Olsen, 2000). Clergy also operate in systems that seem contradictory, which further expounds the impact of fatigue and burnout on their ability to effectively lead. For example, clergy may be tasked by a board of directors to cut the budget while also being pressured by the congregants to hire more staff or start new ministry initiatives (Grosch & Olsen, 2000). When coupled with an unchecked ego, these systemic conflicts may negatively impact an ecclesial leader's decision-making processes. Given this, in later chapters I will show

how 2 Samuel 11:1-27 is a model for how external and internal stress amongst spiritual leaders interacts with moral and ethical decision making.

Stress and burnout have a direct impact on leadership. Furthermore, spiritual leaders, such as clergy, are especially susceptible to compassion fatigue and burnout. The objective of the current study is to identify how stress and burnout, which serve as elements of leadership fatigue, impact moral and ethical leadership. Since, as suggested by past research, burnout and stress not only lead to moral disengagement and emotional exhaustion but they also relate to secondary trauma and PTS, I will build on the literature by linking PTS with leadership fatigue.

Trauma

According to Floyd (2008), trauma is any event that occurs outside of the normal human experience that pushes individuals past their built-in defense mechanisms and stress thresholds. Trauma happens on both internal and external levels (Floyd, 2008). Trauma differs from crisis in that the former is a matter of perception, while the latter is specifically connected to an experience (Floyd, 2008). Floyd suggested, "Following a traumatic event, all individuals experience some symptoms, whether cognitive, emotional, behavioral, spiritual, or relational" ("Symptoms: Concluding Comments," para. 1). There are two types of trauma: single-event trauma (Level-1) and multiple-blow trauma (Level-2; Floyd, 2008). Secondary trauma typically falls under Level-2 trauma (Floyd, 2008). Floyd argued that trauma impacts human information processing, concentration, and emotional response; furthermore, trauma often leads to feelings of numbness, relational withdrawal, anger, sadness, sleep disturbance, and hypervigilance. It is important to note that trauma is also connected with risk taking and weakened spirituality (Floyd, 2008). Although not all trauma survivors experience PTSD, Floyd suggested that almost half of those survivors do develop PTSD. Since King David led in combat and traumatic environments and given the modern research on trauma, this book serves as a bridge between the latest literature on PTS and the experiences of ancient leaders as seen in the life of King David.

Regel and Joseph (2010) suggested that no two individuals respond to traumatic events in the same manner. In fact, more often than not, people return to a sense of normalcy within a few days or weeks of experiencing trauma (Regel & Joseph, 2010). However, in some cases, especially those related to combat, feelings of fear, anxiety, and stress can linger, producing a wide variety of side effects (Regel & Joseph, 2010). These side effects include restlessness, outbursts of anger, fatigue, and antisocial behavior (Regel & Joseph, 2010). According to Regel and Joseph, "There is no right or wrong way" (p. 3) to respond to trauma. Furthermore, Regel and Joseph argued that some people are less resilient to trauma than others due to outside stressors or the compounding factor of previous trauma. Throughout this book, I will consider how the presence of stress and prior traumatic experiences may have affected King David's psychological and physical responses to trauma.

Not all trauma is related to *life or death* situations such as combat. Tanner et al. (2013) suggested that forced termination is a frequently occurring, yet underexplored, cause of trauma. Tanner et al. set out to empirically explore the relationship between PTSD and forced termination by surveying members of the clergy who have experienced the psychological distress of losing their jobs. According to Tanner et al., the "mobbing and psychological harassment" (p. 1291) that leads to clergy forced termination often results in clergy experiencing symptoms correlate with PTSD and generalized anxiety disorder. If the "intrusive demands of ministry" (Tanner et al., 2013, p. 1283), burnout, controlling organizations, and forced pastoral exit produce the symptoms of PTSD in clergy, then one can assume that the role of ecclesial leadership has the potential to be traumatic on a clinical level. Therefore, I believe that the *act* and *role* of leadership, especially within spiritual contexts, may produce trauma.

Williams and Allen (2015) argued that trauma does not always result in negative leadership outcomes. According to Williams and Allen's research into prosocial leadership, "Following trauma, individuals go through the challenging process of recovery" (p. 87). During this recovery process, individuals suffering with trauma often use their experience to assist and comfort others who are also going through a crisis or recovering from trauma (Williams & Allen, 2015). Furthermore, Williams and Allen suggested that high levels of resilience allow individuals dealing with trauma to reframe their struggles with a focus on the *greater good*. The results of Williams and Allen's qualitative inquiry into posttraumatic prosocial leadership revealed that the following themes summarize the positive side of trauma in some leaders: (a) perspective enlargement, (b) resilience to cause rejection, (c) expanded knowledge, (d) self-acknowledgement of ongoing distress, (e) acknowledged encouragement (from others), (f) connection with target recipients, and (g) compassionate connections. Given this, I believe that even though leadership fatigue and trauma may negatively impact the ethical and moral decision-making process, there is still room for leaders to redeem their trauma for positive purposes.

One reason that little is known about the effects of trauma on ethical leadership is the reluctance some institutional review boards have regarding trauma-related research (Jaffe et al., 2015). Due to the sensitive nature of certain traumatic events, such as combat trauma or sexual trauma, it is difficult for researchers to ask interview questions in an ethical, objective, and nonthreatening way (Jaffe et al., 2015). Thus, inquiries into the impact of trauma are full of potential ethical dilemmas (Jaffe et al., 2015). However, according to Jaffe et al. (2015), "Individuals generally find research participation to be a positive experience and do not regret participation, regardless of trauma history or PTSD" (p. 40). Thus, the current study seeks to open the door for future research into the role of trauma by first exploring trauma in an ancient context. This book serves as a bridge linking ancient traumatic experiences with future research.

Posttraumatic Stress

According to the DSM-IV, PTSD includes symptoms of hyperarousal, dysphoria, avoidance, numbing, and a re-experiencing of trauma (Contractor et al., 2013). Contractor et al. (2013) suggested that both the behavioral activation system and the behavioral inhibition system interact with PTSD in a way that could lead an individual toward undesirable behavior in order to avoid certain stimuli. The behavioral activation system "guides behavior toward positive/rewarding situations" (Contractor et al., 2013, p. 645), whereas the behavioral inhibition system guides toward the conflict between reward and punishment. Although there is a wealth of literature on PTS and PTSD, very few studies exist that associate the aforementioned topics with ethical and moral leadership. Since PTSD is an extension of unchecked PTS, I use the current literature on PTS to explore the role of avoidance, numbing, dysphoria, and hyperarousal in ethical decision making.

Koffel et al. (2012) argued that the overlap between PTSD and other anxiety and mood disorders may lead to misdiagnosis, which negatively impacts the patient and the scholarly understanding of PTSD. For example, dysphoria, which is one of the primary symptoms of PTSD, actually relates more to depression and generalized anxiety disorder than it does to PTSD (Koffel et al., 2012). Koffel et al. suggested that deemphasizing dysphoria and emphasizing symptoms specific to PTSD will allow scholars and health care practitioners to better serve those suffering from PTSD. Research into the DSM-5 shows that the symptoms anger, aggressive behavior, and negative expectations closely relate to PTSD (Koffel et al., 2012). However, only anger showed a significant correlation with PTSD (Koffel et al., 2012). Furthermore, test scores reveal that anger increases between predeployment and postdeployment (Koffel et al., 2012). Given this, in future chapters I will compare the attitudes and actions of King David as seen in 2 Samuel 11:1-27 in order to examine how the specific symptoms of PTS/PTSD affect ethical and moral leadership.

Combat leadership almost ensures exposure to stress and trauma. According to Blais and Renshaw (2013), of the 1.9 million soldiers deployed to combat zones in the first 9 years of the Global War on Terror, 94% "report witnessing or personally experiencing a traumatic event" (p. 77), which could lead to the stress and psychological distress associated with burnout/fatigue or PTS. However, most of these cases go undiagnosed due to the stigma associated with PTS and its symptoms (Blais & Renshaw, 2013). Chamberlin (2012) argued that the long historical narrative of PTSD is one in which those suffering from PTS were viewed as being weak, shell-shocked, malingerers, and unmanly. Furthermore, those who suffered from stress, anxiety, or what is now known as PTSD were believed to have been "predisposed to these illnesses due to personal or familial weakness" (p. Chamberlin, 2012, p. 361). Thus, soldiers would rather deal with undiagnosed or untreated PTS than with the emasculating stigma associated with the psychological condition (Blais & Renshaw, 2013; Chamberlin, 2012).

Stigma often takes the form of outside attitudes that are projected onto an individual dealing with PTS (Blais & Renshaw, 2013). However, Blais and Renshaw (2013) suggested that self-stigma is a greater inhibitor of treatment than outside stigma. They revealed, "Service members who reported greater self-stigma reported that they were less likely to seek help for psychological distress" (p. 81). If self-stigma causes one to avoid treatment, and if *saving face* is the fruit of ethical egoism, and if untreated PTS leads to undesirable behavior, then it is possible that the stigma associated with PTS also undercuts ethical and moral leadership. Although King David did not have access to the modern understanding of PTS, as a *man of war* he lived in a masculine-framed context that may have shaped how he dealt with the stress and trauma of combat. Therefore, this book should add value to the current literature regarding stigma and PTS due to its emphasis on how the various elements of combat-related trauma and stress impact behavior and decision making.

It is important to note that PTS is not exclusive to military contexts. In fact, measures such as the PTSD Checklist-Civilian Version (PCL-C) are often used to examine PTSD symptoms in nonclinical and nonmilitary samples (Conybeare et al., 2012). According to Conybeare et al. (2012), "A questionnaire might measure different constructs depending on the type of sample being measured" (p. 699). The PCL-C is *identical* to the PTSD Checklist-Military Version with the exception of items that refer to military trauma (Conybeare et al., 2012). This 17-item instrument measures the avoidance, numbing, hyperarousal, and re-experiencing symptoms associated with PTSD. Although the PCL-C proves that PTS is not restricted to the military context, there is room in the literature to explore the similarities between the impact of PTS on ethical and moral leadership in both military and civilian contexts. Thus, I will juxtapose these contexts in relation to leadership fatigue, PTS, and ethical and moral leadership.

Grossman (2009) stated that killing in combat is not something one does with ease. Studies have shown that when given the option to fight, flee, posture, or submit, soldiers from earliest wars to the modern era typically choose killing as a last resort (Grossman, 2009). This is backed up by the alarming rate of nonfires or overfires in critical battles. For example, in the aftermath of the Battle of Gettysburg during the American Civil War, over 24,000 loaded muskets were recovered from the battlefield, which indicates posturing or intentional nonfires (Grossman, 2009). Thus, in order to kill in combat one must be trained or conditioned to dehumanize, rationalize, or *block out* in order to take the life of an enemy (Grossman, 2009). Furthermore, the longer individuals are exposed to combat conditions, the more likely they are to experience emotional exhaustion, which further inhibits the decision-making process (Grossman, 2009). According to Grossman, studying killing in combat is like "virgins studying sex" (p. 1) in that most people will never truly experience what it is to take a life in combat. One could argue that studying ethics is also like *virgins studying sex* since the human condition often runs counter to what is truly ethical and moral (Grossman, 2009).

Grossman and Christensen (2012) argued, "There are only two kinds of people . . . [on the battlefield:] warriors and victims" ("Introduction: The New Warriors," para. 4). However, the brutality of combat often causes the *warrior* to become a victim of psychological and emotional trauma that negatively impacts every area of his or her life (Grossman & Christensen, 2012). According to Grossman and Christensen, "When it is another human being who causes our fear, pain and suffering, it shatters, destroys, and devastates us" ("Universal Human Phobia," para. 11). Thus, the insomnia, hormonal imbalances, mood swings, and dark thoughts associated with PTS have a profound impact on a warrior's ability to cope with combat (Grossman & Christensen, 2012). For example, after 24 hours of sleep deprivation, a person reaches the "physiological and psychological equivalent of being legally drunk" (Grossman & Christensen, 2012, "The Equivalent," para. 1). This book explores how prolonged combat, much killing, and emotional exhaustion impact the ethical and moral leadership of King David as seen in 2 Samuel 11:1-27.

Fear, anger, and dysphoria are not the only feelings associated with PTSD. For example, Harman and Lee (2010) revealed that feelings of shame may cause an individual to process prior trauma as an ongoing threat, which further exacerbates the other feelings associated with PTSD. According to Harman and Lee, shame is "shown to have a significant positive correlation with self-criticism and a significant negative correlation with self-reassurance" (p. 21). Thus, feelings of shame cause individuals to doubt their own ability to recover from or move beyond their trauma. Moreover, since these individuals are "unable to defend themselves from their own self-critical attacks" (Harman & Lee, 2010, p. 16), feelings of defeat "maintain" (p. 16) the PTS condition. Therefore, if trauma produces shame, which leads to a form of self-criticism and a lack of self-assurance I will explore the role of trauma and shame in King David's unethical decision making as seen in 2 Samuel 11:1-27.

Prior experience with treatment also plays a role in how one copes with PTSD (Reger et al., 2013). According to Reger et al. (2013), soldiers who have prior experience with mental health care are more likely to seek treatment, including psychotherapy and pharmacological therapy, than those who have no experience with mental health care. This difference is due to factors such as stigma, fear of career damage, and concern regarding the side effects of pharmaceutical treatment in combat (Reger et al., 2013). Thus, deployed soldiers who are suffering from PTSD may refuse treatment, which further disturbs the decision-making process. Furthermore, Reger et al. argued that soldiers prefer exposure-based therapy, which involves confronting the source of trauma, over medicinal-based therapies for the treatment of PTSD. Given this, I will add to the literature by linking what is now known about preferences for treatment with avoidance and *cover-up* as they relate to ethical and moral decision making in combat leadership environments.

Skogstad et al. (2013) conducted a study of PTSD in workplace environments, which has implications for the current study on ethical and moral leadership. The Skogstad et al. in-depth literature review explored PTSD and others-focused vocations such as law enforcement, emergency medical technicians, postal workers, and firefighters. Skogstad et al. revealed, "Mental health problems prior to the traumatic event and weak social support increase the risk of PTSD" (p. 175). Specifically, they revealed that resilience, vulnerability, and neuroticism are better predictors of PTSD than the frequency or severity of a traumatic event (Skogstad et al., 2013). Hence, this book explores the previous mental state of King David in order to deduce how resilience, vulnerability, or neuroticism may have impacted his leadership.

Some have suggested that repeated exposure to combat puts one at great risk of developing PTS and PTSD symptoms (Sundin et al., 2010). Sundin et al. (2010) conducted an in-depth review of the prevalence of PTSD in soldiers deployed during combat operations in Iraq. According to Sundin et al., "PTSD prevalence increases over the 12 months following deployment" (p. 379) for U.S. soldiers. However, they also revealed a lower prevalence of PTSD in United Kingdom soldiers (Sundin et al., 2010). Thus, more research is needed to reconcile the perceived contradictions and conflict in the literature regarding the prevalence of PTSD in combat-exposed troops

(Sundin et al., 2010). This book fills the gap by exploring the effects of PTSD with previously underused methodologies such as sociorhetorical analysis.

Exposure to trauma does not guarantee that one will develop PTSD (DiGangi et al., 2013). Moreover, researchers have not yet compiled an exhaustive list of PTSD symptoms or predictors (DiGangi et al., 2013). However, DiGangi et al. (2013) argued, "Pre-trauma characteristics historically thought to be symptoms may predict PTSD" (p. 728). According to DiGangi et al., these characteristics include one's (a) coping abilities, (b) response styles, (c) personality, (d) psychopathology, (e) psychophysiological factors, and (f) social ecological factors. DiGangi et al. also pointed to ancient literature such as *The Epic of Gilgamesh* to demonstrate the complexity involved in pretrauma experiences and posttraumatic responses. Thus, I will build on the DiGangi et al. research by using ancient literature to explore both pretrauma risk factors and posttraumatic response as they relate to ethical and moral leadership behaviors.

As stated, very few studies have addressed the psychological state of King David, especially as it relates to combat trauma. However, Ruthven and Ruthven's (2001) research into major depressive disorder (MDD) offers insight into the mental health of King David. The symptoms of MDD include (a) depressed mood, (b) lack of interest in normal activities, (c) dramatic weight loss/gain, (d) insomnia, (e) physical agitation, (f) general fatigue, (g) excessive feelings of guilt, (h) loss of concentration and indecisiveness, and (i) suicidal thoughts (Ruthven & Ruthven, 2001). According to Ruthven and Ruthven, "David's MDD may also be inferred from the Bathsheba affair . . . [since] the deliberate, aggressive nature of such a sexual affair is invigorating; it lashes out against the boring pain of depression and provides sensate, experiential proof of being alive." (p. 430) Moreover, David's *failure* to join the armies of Israel in battle demonstrated a lack of interest in normal activities, and his pacing on the roof during the evening demonstrated sleeplessness and "psychomotor agitation" (Ruthven & Ruthven, 2001, p. 429)—all of which are symptoms of MDD. Therefore, I will expand on Ruthven and Ruthven's work by combining the symptoms of PTS, burnout, and compassion fatigue into the concept of leadership fatigue. Furthermore, I will explore the various underlying causes behind David's diminished mental state in 2 Samuel 11:1-27.

Trauma, burnout, and stress are proven to impact one's ability to function in high-stress environments. PTS and PTSD are complex concepts with a variety of risk factors, both of which negatively impact an individual's quality of life. The objective of the study presented in this book is to explore how leadership fatigue, which includes elements of PTSD, trauma, stress, and burnout, interacts with ethical and moral leadership in the life and decisions of a leader. Based on the evidence, there is much to learn about how PTSD affects values-based leadership. Furthermore, since PTSD occurs in both noncombat and combat environments, and since King David served as both a warrior and an executive leader, and since little is known about how pretrauma and posttrauma affect leadership ethics, it is appropriate to explore these concepts through robust exegetical methodologies. Therefore, I will examine leadership fatigue and its impact on ethical and moral failure through a sociorhetorical analysis of 2 Samuel 11:1-27.

According to Rae (2009), Christian leaders tend to be "deontologically oriented" (p. 17) since the moral commands of God as found within the Hebrew and Christian Scriptures serve as the framework for the *divine command theory* that supports ethical behavior in Christian leadership. If the Hebrew and Christian Scriptures are the guidebook for Christian ethical and moral behavior, why would a Christian leader act in a way that is contrary to his or her fundamental beliefs? The answer may be found by connecting what is known about ethical and moral leadership with what is known about trauma, burnout, and compassion fatigue. Since ethical and moral leadership are often related to the divine commands found within religious texts such as the Bible (Rae, 2009); and since unethical and immoral behavior often stem from prioritizing self-interests (Northouse, 2015); and since workplace stress, burnout, and PTS all connect with marked behavioral changes (Diestel et al., 2013), one could argue that the Bible may serve as a valuable resource for the exploration of leadership fatigue and ethical and moral leadership.

CHAPTER 3

What's So Good About The Good Book?

There is a great need for varied methodologies in the exploration of ethical and moral leadership as they relate to trauma and stress. Since values-based ethics is often connected with sacred texts like the Bible, it is necessary to explore ethical and moral behavior through the lens of theology (Rae, 2009). As the queen of the sciences, theology as explored through exegetical methodologies provides researchers with a process for "thinking about life" (Stone & Duke, 2013, p. 3) in a way that differs from traditional quantitative methodologies. Moreover, qualitative methodologies such as hermeneutical phenomenology and sociorhetorical analysis lend themselves to the exploration of essences and meaning in a way that considers the various layers of one's personal experience, whereas quantitative methodologies function within the strict and objective confines of prescribed instrumentation (Patton, 2002; Robbins, 1996a).

Because character, morality, ethics, spirituality, and ontology address the inner issues of leadership, it is important to utilize data and methodologies that also focus on issues of personhood and being (Crowther, 2012b). In fact, several recent leadership studies have utilized the Hebrew and Christian Scriptures as the data source for sociorhetorical exploration into authentic leadership, transformational leadership, servant leadership, follower development, and ethical leadership (Crowther, 2012a; Henson, 2015; Huizing, 2013; Perry, 2016). Furthermore, much has been written about what a leader should *do*, while in-depth studies into *how* and *why* leaders behave ethically and morally are limited at best (Brown & Treviño, 2006). Brown and Treviño (2006) proposed that a high level of moral reasoning "positively relates to ethical leadership . . . [and] internal locus of control is positively related to ethical leadership" (p. 605). Therefore, it is important to explore these propositions along with the established gap in the current research by using the Hebrew and Christian Scriptures as the primary source of data.

The next few chapters address one primary problem: the epidemic of moral and ethical failure amongst executive level leaders. A deeper understanding of *why* leaders may make unethical and immoral decisions could enhance leadership development processes in a way that reverses the trend of rapid ethical and moral failure. These results could benefit both secular and Christian organizational leadership paradigms.

The Hebrew and Christian Scriptures are a proven source for insight into moral and ethical behavior. According to Stone and Duke (2013), the Christian faith is a "way of living" (p. 38) guided my moral values expressed as Christian ethics. Thus, all of the theological writings found within the Hebrew and Christian Scriptures have ethical implications (Stone & Duke, 2013). Moreover, since *being* a Christian involves "upholding certain ethical principles and ideals" (Stone & Duke, 2013, p. 15), it is important for Christian leaders to have an understanding of how theology, ethics, and morality intersect in the decision-making processes of a leader. Stone and Duke argued that although the Christian sacred text known as the Bible is historically based, one should not reduce the exploration of the Bible to historical research methodologies. In order to properly employ sound interpretive principles such as biblical hermeneutics, one should be *intentional* about how one treats the sacred text (Stone & Duke, 2013). According to Patton (2002) "Hermeneutics focuses on the problem of interpretation" (p. 114) while providing a "theoretical framework" (p. 114) for extracting meaning from a text. Rather than reading meaning into a text, hermeneutics allows the qualitative researcher to draw meaning out of the original linguistic, social, and cultural context of the text (Patton, 2002; Robbins, 1996a).

It is important to note that hermeneutics differs from traditional empiricism in that the former provides an *interpretation* of meaning while the latter focuses on concrete and objective claims (Patton, 2002). Robbins' (1996a) sociorhetorical analysis is one type of hermeneutical methodology that allows researchers to search for meaning by approaching the text from a variety of *angles*. Sociorhetorical analysis explores the historical, cultural, social, ideological, and linguistic layers of the text in search of meaning (Robbins, 1996a). Robbins suggested, "Like an intricately woven tapestry, a text contains complex patterns and images" (p. 2). Thus, multiple scholars have employed sociorhetorical analysis to study the Hebrew and Christian Scriptures in conjunction with ethics, morality, and leadership.

For example, Huizing (2013) conducted a sociorhetorical analysis of Leviticus 23 as seen in the complete works of the Apostle Paul in order to examine the role of ritual in follower development. Huizing revealed several connections with ethical leadership. According to Huizing, "The very idea of ethical goodness requires a high degree of authenticity" (p. 29). Furthermore, follower actions do not necessarily rely on the actions of ethical or unethical leaders, since true ethical goodness "is measured by the follower's own responses" (Huizing, 2013, p. 30). Therefore, it is critical to develop authentic, effective, and ethical followers by making *lived-out* ethics an integral part of organizational ritual (Huizing, 2013).

Like Huizing (2013), Perry (2016) also used sociorhetorical analysis to explore the Christian Scriptures in connection with organizational leadership theory. While Huizing revealed connections to ethical leadership, Perry intentionally sought to examine ethical leadership as seen in 1 Timothy 3-4. Perry showed (a) ethical leadership is contextually formed, (b) virtue and ethics are not mutually exclusive, (c) ethical leadership is concerned with individual and organizational effectiveness, and (d) ethical leadership involves modeling for empowerment. According to Perry, much of the existing literature on ethical leadership lacks a theological understanding; moreover, "for leaders to be ethical, they must engage in holistic evaluation of their contexts" (p. 80). Since the Hebrew and Christian Scriptures are appropriate sources for the study of ethical and moral leadership, and since qualitative methodologies are best suited for exploring the meaning of written texts, and since previous research proves that sociorhetorical analysis is an effective tool for exploring ethical themes as seen in the Bible, I use exegetical methodologies to further examine ethical leadership as seen in 2 Samuel 11:1-27.

Ethical leadership is central to both the role and act of leadership (Bass, 2009). Within ethical leadership is the foundational construct of morality, which influences the thoughts, beliefs, values, and behaviors of the ethical leader (Rae, 2009). Furthermore, the altruistic and moral reasoning components of ethical leadership connect to spiritual leadership theory, authentic leadership theory, transformational leadership theory, and servant leadership theory (Avolio & Gardner, 2005; Bass, 2009; Burns 1978; Patterson, 2003; Rae, 2009). Thus, one could argue that ethical leadership and moral leadership serve as the foundation for values-based leadership theories. Moreover, one could argue that a study of ethical leadership should benefit the entire field of organizational leadership. However, a review of the current literature on ethical and moral leadership revealed a significant gap regarding the impact of trauma, burnout, and stress on ethical and moral decision making and behavior. Much of the literature on PTS, burnout, and trauma has focused on symptomatic behaviors (Diaconescu, 2015; Maslach et al., 2001; Regel & Joseph, 2010). However, very little research has considered the role or act of leading as being traumatic in and of itself. Furthermore, few studies have attempted to connect leadership fatigue to ethical and moral decision making.

The story of King David and Bathsheba found within 2 Samuel 11 involves combat, PTS-like symptoms, and several leadership decisions, which should offer insight into the various ways that leadership fatigue influences ethical and moral leadership. Since the Bible reveals the moral character of God (Rae, 2009,; and since the story of David found in 2 Samuel 11:1-27 involves multiple genres and textual layers (Finkelstein & Silberman; Yee, 1988), and since qualitative methodologies are well suited for in-depth research into written texts (Patton, 2002), it is appropriate to use sociorhetorical analysis to extract meaning from 2 Samuel 11:1-27. This robust methodology allows the current study to consider ethical and moral leadership from a historical, theological, and narratological perspective. Furthermore, as a proven scientific method for the exploration of sacred texts as they relate to values-based leadership, the use of sociorhetorical analysis in this book further substantiates the Hebrew and Christian Scriptures as being valuable sources of information for organizational leadership research.

CHAPTER 4

Sociorhetorical Analysis: Exploring the Texture of Texts

Robbins' (1996a,1996b) sociorhetorical analysis is a qualitative methodology that uses biblical exegesis to explore the semantic, social and cultural, historic, ideological, and theological layers of a text. This multilayered approach to classic hermeneutics involves the examination of the following textual *layers*: inner textual analysis, intertexture analysis, social and cultural analysis, ideological analysis, and sacred texture analysis (Robbins, 1996b). This method is robust in that it does not impose the will of the researcher onto the historical text but, instead, seeks to first find meaning by answering the question, What does it mean in its context? (Osborne, 2006; Robbins, 1996b). Rather than read 21st-century meaning into a biblical character or New testament principles into Old Testament contexts, this study uses sociorhetorical analysis to use the language and culture of King David as a bridge toward the current understanding of ethical and moral leadership as they relate to trauma and stress (Osborne, 2006). Since the Old Testament has a prominent and, in many cases, a symbiotic relationship with the texts, customs, and culture of the Ancient Near East (ANE), sociorhetorical analysis provides the researcher with the multiple tools to explore the aforementioned relationships (Merrill, Rooker, & Grisanti, 2011; Walton, 2006). This methodology is especially important since the "validity of reason, the importance of history, the worth of the individual, and the reality of nature" (Oswalt, 2009, "The Biblical Worldview," para. 2) prove that a link exists between Israelite and Greek thought and the current understanding of ethics and morality. Thus, sociorhetorical analysis within the context of this study seeks to validate hermeneutics as both a discipline and a foundational element of "all intellectual endeavors" (Vanhoozer, 2009, p.19). Therefore, sociorhetorical analysis is relevant for this look into the life of David because of its robust exegetical treatment of sacred texts, its proven effectiveness in previous research, and its foundation in qualitative research methodologies.

The Hebrew and Christian Scriptures were not written on an *island* of isolation. In order to extract meaning from these sacred texts, one must employ appropriate methodologies that consider the role of culture, history, language, and ideology on a particular text. Sociorhetorical analysis is a *multidimensional* and *multi-hermeneutical* approach to texts that allows the researcher to reconcile the tensions between ancient meaning and modern context (Robbins, 1999). According to deSilva (2004), the Old Testament is a foundational group of texts that directly influenced the early construct of Christian leadership as seen in the New Testament. deSilva argued, "The goal of sociorhetorical interpretation is to enter as fully as possible" (p. 23) into the *world* of a text in order to connect the ancient with the present. The *art* and *science* of hermeneutics focuses on the "discovery of historical meaning as intended by the author" (Hernando, 2005, p. 23) as well as how the original audience understood and applied the author's meaning in his or her historical context (Osborne, 2006). Osborne (2006) stated that although biblical interpretation starts with exegesis, the hermeneutical process is not truly complete until one contextualizes and connects the *meaning of the past* with the *meaning for today*. However, since the researcher is the primary instrument in qualitative hermeneutic methodologies such as sociorhetorical analysis, it is important to consider how the researcher's bias shapes the interpretation of meaning (Osborne, 2006; Patton, 2002).

For example, Gerhart (1989) developed a theory of narrative to bolster the use of literary critical analysis in biblical scholarship, which offers insight into the current study's hermeneutical framework. Gerhart's theory proposes that "(1) Narrative is generically cognitive; (2) narrative is generically historical; (3) narrative is generically theological" (p. 13). *Generically cognitive* means that the interpretation of a narrative depends on one's capacity for understanding *how* to read and follow a story (Gerhart, 1989). *Generically historical* means that the interpretation of a narrative must begin with an awareness of how present context *fights* with the *world* of the narrative (Gerhart, 1989). According to Gerhart, "A classic not only says what it says, but all that has and will be said as well" (p. 19). *Generically theological* refers to the way in which narrative forms meaning, which subsequently shapes and forms values and understanding (Gerhart, 1989). Gerhart argued, "A biblical scholar cannot not engage in implicit theological reflection" (p. 21) because of the *inherent* doctrinal lenses through which one reads the Bible. However, this does not mean that narrative cannot stand alone as a pure expression of "God's self-manifestation" (Gerhart, 1989, p. 21). Since *socio* refers to the role of sociology and anthropology in interpretation and *rhetorical* refers to the various ways in which the use of language impacts meaning, one could argue that sociorhetorical criticism is an ideal methodology for studying the narrative of David found in 2 Samuel 11:1-27 (Robbins, 1996a). Given this, I use sociorhetorical analysis to isolate the narrative of 2 Samuel 11:1-27, thus furthering the use of literary critical analysis in biblical scholarship.

As stated, when studying the Hebrew Scriptures, one must consider the role of theology on interpretation. Vanhoozer (2009) argued that since theology flows from biblical interpretation, it is paramount for biblical researchers to use sound hermeneutic principles when making theological assumptions about a text. According to Oswalt (2009), logic and science "cannot stand on their own" ("The Biblical Worldview," para. 1) because neither are self-evident. Both logic and science stem from certain philosophical and theological principles that build the platform for scientific argument (Oswalt, 2009; Walton, 2006). Thus, I argue from a philosophical and theological position that presents the Hebrew and Christian Scriptures as the ultimate source of all that is truly moral and ethical. Furthermore, I believe that the Hebrew and Christian Scriptures "contain truth that transcends time and space and therefore informs our decisions today" (Meadors & Kaiser, 2009, "Introduction," para. 1). Thus, I use sociorhetorical analysis in the upcoming chapters to thoroughly address the immediate context of 2 Samuel 11:1-27 while also *going beyond* the immediate context in order to apply the meaning of 2 Samuel 11:1-27 to modern applications of ethical and moral leadership and their relationship to leadership fatigue and trauma.

Sociorhetorical Analysis

According to Robbins (1996b), sociorhetorical analysis demands that interpreters view human reality, religious belief and practice, and experiences through multiple textual layers and approaches. Sociorhetorical interpretation emerged in the 1970s and 1980s as a tool for integrating sociology, anthropology, and rhetoric as seen in the Gospel of Mark (Robbins, 2004). In the 1990s, sociorhetorical analysis evolved from a tool that explored rhetorical argumentation into an "interpretive analytic" (Robbins, 2004, p. 1). Today, sociorhetorical analysis is a proven instrument for the exploration of leadership principles found within the Hebrew and Christian Scriptures (Crowther, 2012a; Henson, 2015; Huizing, 2013). Sociorhetorical analysis uses five textual approaches: (a) inner texture, (b), intertexture, (c) social and cultural texture, (d) ideological texture, and (e) sacred texture (Robbins, 1996b). According to Robbins (1996b), "One of the goals of a sociorhetorical approach is to set specialized areas of analysis in conversation with one another" (p. 3). Thus, I wish to *create a conversation* between hermeneutics, social psychology, theology, and organizational leadership.

Inner Texture Analysis

Inner texture analysis involves the exploration of syntax and semantics in order to uncover meaning within a text. According to Robbins (1996b), the "relationships among word-phrase and Narrational patterns . . . are the context for the 'networks of signification' in a text" (p. 46). Robbins (1996a) argued that in order to truly examine the meaning of a text, it is often important to "remove all meanings from the text" (p. 7) by first analyzing the basic sense of words and phrases. Thus, inner texture analysis views *words* as instruments of communication that set the stage for uncovering meaning (Robbins, 1996a). The inner texture of 2 Samuel 11:1-27 contains several repeated word patterns and phrases that offer insight into the objectives of the current study. According Robbins (1996b), there are five types of inner texture: (a) repetitive–progressive, (b) opening–middle–closing, (c) narrational, (d) argumentative texture, and (e) sensory–aesthetic texture.

    Repetitive–progressive texture. According to Robbins (1996a), repetitive–progressive texture exists any time a word or phrase is used more than once in a text. This repetition is often a *signal* as to the overall or important themes of the text (Robbins, 1996a). Robbins argued, "Progression emerges out of repetition" (p. 10). An example of repetition–progressive texture is found in the use of *sent* in the passage, which offers insight into King David's ethical leadership behavior.

Opening–middle–closing. Opening–middle–closing texture is concerned with the way in which "plotted time and story time" (Robbins, 1996b, p. 50) frame the *world* of a narrative. Moreover, in the same way that progression emerges out of repetition, the analysis of opening–middle–closing texture sets the stage for the analysis of narrational and sensory–aesthetic texture (Robbins, 1996b). Since I am concerned with the de-evolution of morality in King David's leadership, an examination of the opening–middle–texture should produce data that explains the *why* behind unethical behavior.

Narrational texture. According to Robbins (1996a), "narrational texture resides in voices" (p. 15). These *voices* are often the main characters of the narrative, which add insight into the perspective and meaning of a text (Robbins, 1996a). It is important to note that narrational texture often connects to repetitive–progressive texture in that certain repeated phrases or words advance the story forward in a way that uncovers meaning (Robbins, 1996a). The multiple voices within the 2 Samuel 11:1-27 narrative offer the provide the researcher with a *360-degree* perspective of the impact of unethical and immoral leadership.

Argumentative texture. Robbins (2008) suggested that authors often construct a "context of communication" (p. 81) that produces graphic images in the mind of the reader that both persuades and provides meaning. According to Robbins (1996b), one of the most common forms of argumentative texture is logical reasoning, which often takes the form of *if/then* statements. However, argumentative texture also takes the form of counterarguments presented throughout the narrative that may not appear as obvious as *if/then* statements (Robbins, 1996a). The counterarguments to two of King David's unethical decisions as seen in 2 Samuel 11:1-27 offer insight into the psychological and moral condition of the Israelite King (Garsiel, 1993).

Sensory–aesthetic texture. The sensory–aesthetic texture of a text is concerned with how the author appeals to various senses (e.g., smell, hearing, touch, humor, intuition, sight, and imagination) in order to "provide tone and perhaps color to the discourse" (Robbins, 1996a, p. 30). In 2 Samuel 11:1-27, the author mentions the time of the year and the time of the day and uses emotionally descriptive language to explain the context of King David's leadership.

Intertexture Analysis

Intertexture analysis is concerned with the use of *texts within a text* or the various ways in which the world outside of the text informs the meaning of the text (Robbins, 1996a, 1996b). According to Robbins (1996b), "Every text is a rewriting of other texts, an intertextual activity" (p. 30). However, Camp (2011) suggested that not every instance of intertextual activity is intentional. Nevertheless, numerous connections exist between 2 Samuel 11:1-27, the rest of the Hebrew Scriptures, and the Christian Scriptures (Camp, 2011). According to Robbins (1996a), there are four types of intertextures: (a) oral–scribal, (b) cultural, (c) social, and (d) historical.

    Oral–scribal texture. Robbins (1996b) stated that oral–scribal texture analysis "includes: recitation, recontextualization, and reconfiguration of other texts" (p. 97) within a text. Recitation refers to the direct or indirect conveyance of an oral or written tradition within a text, which is typically prefaced by the phrases *have you not read* or *it is written* (Robbins, 1996a). Conversely, recontextualization refers to the use of words from other texts without explicitly stating that those words are written elsewhere (Robbins, 1996a). Reconfiguration refers to the recounting of an event in a way that causes a *new* event to "outshine" (Robbins, 1996a, p. 50) or "foreshadow" (p. 50) the previous event. Recontextualization and reconfiguration are found in how the author of 2 Samuel 11:1-27 directly referenced Judges 9:50-57 (Sternberg, 1987).

    Cultural intertexture. According to Robbins (1996a), cultural intertexture refers to "insider knowledge" (p. 58), which is known only by those who have had some type of interaction with a culture. This *cultural knowledge* includes values, codes, and scripts (Robbins, 1996a). Cultural intertexture takes the form of echo or reference/allusion (Robbins, 1996a). In 2 Samuel 11:1, the narrative refers to a *rhythm of deployment* for ancient kings, which offers insight into King David's leadership.

    Social intertexture. Like cultural intertexture, social intertexture includes material related to codes, values, norms, and scripts (Robbins, 1996a). However, social intertexture focuses primarily on the observed social knowledge within a culture such as social codes, social identity, social institutions, and social relationships (Robbins, 1996a). 2 Samuel 11:1-27 includes *social knowledge* about royal protocol, family customs, social gatherings, and military traditions.

Historical intertexture. Robbins (1996b) stated, "Historical intertexture differs from social intertexture by its focus on a particular event or period of time rather than social practices that occur regularly as events in one's life" (p. 118) Therefore, within sociorhetorical analysis, the term *historical* refers to specific events (Robbins, 1996a). Although the opening verse of 2 Samuel 11 refers to cultural and social texture, it also mentions a specific battle during a specific time in history.

Social and Cultural Texture

According to Robbins (1996b), "Every meaning has a context" (p. 144). Thus, social and cultural texture analysis involves the exploration of the social and cultural nature of the text itself (Robbins, 1996a). The primary difference between social and cultural texture analysis and intertexture analysis is that the former makes use of anthropological and sociological theory in order to make social and cultural sense out of the *voices* within a text (Robbins, 1996b). Social and cultural texture allow the researcher to investigate the various ways by which a text attempts to "encourage its readers to adopt certain social and cultural locations and orientations rather than others" (Robbins, 1996a, p. 72).

Specific social topics. Robbins (1996a) suggested religious texts often *speak* from a specific worldview for the purpose of eliciting a social response. Robbins summarized those social responses as (a) conversionist, (b) revolutionist, (c) introversionist, (d) gnostic–manipulationist, (e) thaumaturgical, (f) reformist, and (g) utopian. Since 2 Samuel 11:1-27 predates much the philosophical underpinnings of the *special social topics*, the current study is best served by avoiding this area of social and cultural texture. Furthermore, scholars have agreed that 2 Samuel 11:1-27 is intentionally vague in its presentation of a worldview in order to force readers to come to their own conclusions regarding *good* and *evil* (Garsiel, 1993; Sternberg, 1987).

Common social and cultural topics. According to Robbins (1996a), "Common social and cultural topics are the overall environment for the specific social topics in a text" (p. 75). The use of this texture allows the research to avoid the mistake of *reading into* the past by making assumptions about cultural and societal norms that were not present in the ANE

(Robbins, 1996a). Topics within this texture include (a) honor, guilt/shame, and rights; (b) dyadic and individualist personalities; (c) dyadic and legal contracts and agreements; (d) challenge–response (riposte); (e) economic exchange systems; (f), overabundant, insufficient, or limited goods; and (g) purity codes (Robbins, 1996a). Several common and social topics are connected to 2 Samuel 11:1-27, such as the dynamics of honor, shame, and rights found in Bathsheba's submission to King David's sexual advances (Abasili, 2011).

Final cultural categories. This subtexture deals with the manner in which the text presents its arguments (Robbins, 1996a). According to Robbins (1996a), these rhetorical arguments take the form of dominant culture rhetoric, subculture rhetoric, counter culture rhetoric, and contraculture rhetoric. As with *special social topics,* this subtexture depends on philosophical principles that were not yet articulated during the writing of 2 Samuel 11:1-27. However, some have suggested that the author did in fact manipulate the narrative in a way that challenges the dominant culture of the ANE (Garsiel, 1993; Greenberg, 2003; Sternberg, 1987).

Ideological Analysis

Ideological analysis is primarily concerned with *people* (Robbins, 1996b). Robbins (1996b) argued, "Every theology has a politics" (p. 192), which suggests that a series of agreements and disagreements take place between the author, the audience, and the reader (Robbins, 1996a). According to Robbins (1996a), in order to conduct an ideological analysis, the researcher must first identify and analyze his or her own presuppositions and ideologies. Next, the researcher must compare and contrast his or her own ideologies as they relate to various groups (Robbins, 1996a). After this, the researcher must adopt "a mode of theological, historical, sociological, anthropological, psychological, or literary discourse" (Robbins, 1996a, p. 106) in the text. Finally, the researcher must examine the various spheres of ideology within the text such as the ideology in the social and cultural location of the implied author—the ideology of power in the text (Robbins, 1996a). The use of power is a central issue in the 2 Samuel 11 narrative.

Sacred Texture Analysis

Robbins (1996a) suggested that sacred texture connects to all of the other textures within sociorhetorical analysis methods. Sacred texture analysis involves the exploration of the divine within the text and the ways by which the divine interacts with humanity (Robbins, 1996a). Sacred texture analysis includes at least one of the following categories: (a) deity, (b) holy persons, (c) spirit beings, (d) divine history, (e) human redemption, (f) human commitment, (g) religious communities, and (h) ethics (Robbins, 1996a). The final verse of 2 Samuel 11 connects the entire passage to deity and divine history. Moreover, the entire passage contains multiple ethical issues.

Sociorhetorical analysis allows the researcher to take a multi layered view of a text with the purpose of extracting meaning (Robbins, 1996b). Furthermore, sociorhetorical analysis allows the researcher to engage multiple areas of analysis at the same time (Robbins, 1996b). This systematic approach to hermeneutics not only provides the researcher with the necessary rigor to counter bias, it also allows the researcher to *enter into* the world of the text and return with meaning for present leadership contexts (House & Aditya, 1997; Patton, 2002; Robbins, 1996a).

Okay, now that we have firmly built the case for the value of ethical and moral leadership, the reality of leadership fatigue, and the relevance of the Bible as a source for research, it is time to dig into 2 Samuel 11...right after we talk about King David and review the direction of the study.

CHAPTER 5

David of Bethlehem and the Direction of the Study

This study presented in this book fills a critical gap in the literature by answering the *why* questions relating to ethical and moral leadership. Research questions serve as both the foundation and the compass for qualitative exploration (Patton, 2002). The current study asks the following questions:

1. What moral and ethical decisions did David make in 2 Samuel 11:1-27?
2. Why did David make these decisions?
3. What prior trauma or stress influenced David's decisions?
4. Does this pericope offer insight into modern ethical and moral leadership theories?
5. Are there implications for Christian leadership found within this pericope?

Significance of the Study

This study is significant in several ways. First, this study addresses a critical gap in the literature regarding the interplay between trauma and stress and moral and ethical leadership. Although scholars and practitioners have long called for moral and ethical leaders, the topics have only been addressed in the literature formally over the past 25 years (Rhode, 2006). This is in spite of the fact that ethical leaders are frequently rated as being more effective, hard working, trusting, and connected with employee job satisfaction, positive organizational outcomes, and healthy organizational climates (Johnson, 2013). Furthermore, this study may expand the current understanding of combat-based trauma on leadership by focusing on the role of moral development in ethical decision making. Although PTS addresses a series of symptoms, it does not adequately address the human condition or the consequences of moral injury on leadership behavior (Tick, 2014). This study should advance organizational leadership theory by filling the aforementioned gaps.

Second, this study is the first exhaustive study of 2 Samuel 11:1-27. David is a frequently praised biblical leader whose narrative connects in some way from the Book of Ruth to the Book of Revelation (Berger, 2009; Finkelstein & Silberman, 2007). The fact that his greatest sin is openly recorded in Scripture should not be taken lightly (Greenberg, 2003). However, most of the literature connected to this pericope has not explored the multiple textual layers found within the passage. By addressing the linguistic, social and cultural, ideological, historical, and theological layers of 2 Samuel 11:1-27 through sociorhetorical analysis, this study should advance theory by providing new insights into an ancient text. Moreover, this study should further substantiate exegetical methodologies as being a valid and reliable instrument for the qualitative exploration of organizational leadership theory.

Finally, this study may offer insight into how a leader's past experiences impact future decisions. By studying David as both warrior and king, this study may provide current and future leaders with a framework for how moral development shapes ethical decision making and behavior. This is relevant since both combat and workplace stress seem to connect to moral and ethical processes (Diaconescu, 2015; Grossman, 2009; Grossman & Christensen, 2012; Hendron et al., 2012, 2014). Therefore, this study should advance ethical and moral leadership theory by providing new insight into the *why* behind ethical and moral decision making and behavior in the context of leadership.

Scope and Limitations

This study explores 2 Samuel 11:1-27 by way of sociorhetorical analysis. Although it is beyond the scope of this study to exhaustively explore other biblical passages, the nature of the sociorhetorical analysis allows for the inclusion of other texts, especially in the *intertexture* analysis phase (Robbins, 1996a). It is also beyond the scope of this study to explore other values-based leadership theories such as servant leadership, authentic leadership, spiritual leadership, and transformational leadership. Thus, the analysis and discussion within this study emerges from the theoretical framework of ethical leadership, moral leadership, trauma-related stress, and a sociorhetorical analysis of 2 Samuel 11:1-27. The biggest limitation of this study is the use of qualitative hermeneutical methodologies. Qualitative research lends itself to bias in that the primary instrument is the actual researcher (Patton, 2002). However, the rigor of sociorhetorical analysis and the validity of exegetical methodologies within the literature help to counter this limitation (Crowther, 2012a; Henson, 2015; Huizing, 2013).

Definition of Terms

Ethical leadership is defined as "the demonstration of normatively appropriate conduct through personal actions and interpersonal relationships, and the promotion of such conduct to followers through two-way communication, reinforcement, and decision-making" (Brown, Treviño, & Harrison, 2005, p. 120). Ethical leadership involves a moral base that influences the ethical decision making and behavioral processes of a leader (Brown & Mitchell, 2010; Brown. Treviño, et al., 2005; Rae, 2009). Although the two terms are often used interchangeably, moral leadership is not the same as ethical leadership.

Leadership fatigue refers to the combination of internal and external trauma, work-related stress, and morally intense situations and their effect on a leader's decision making and behavioral processes (DiGangi et al., 2013; Hendron et al., 2012, 2014; Zheng et al., 2015). Accordingly, leadership fatigue influences a leader's behaviors and thought processes (Zheng et al., 2015). Therefore, this study uses the term leadership fatigue to encapsulate workplace stress, burnout, and compassion fatigue within the context of organizational leadership.

Moral leadership refers to the underlying values base that frames one's core beliefs, thoughts, and subsequent actions (Brown & Mitchell, 2010; Rae, 2009; Rhode, 2006). Moral leadership is the *compass* that not only guides an individual's sense of right or wrong, it also influences organizational behavior, design, and development (Becker, 2009, pp. 14-15). Thus, moral leadership forms the foundation for ethical leadership.

Posttraumatic stress refers to the normal psychological and physiological response one has to experiencing a traumatic event (Regel & Joseph, 2010). This response includes sleeplessness, anxiety, hyper-awareness, guilt, vivid memories of the traumatic event, withdrawal, and emotional outbursts (Regel & Joseph, 2010). Within the term PTS are the terms *trauma* and *stress*. Trauma is an emotional or physical wound brought about by a certain event or experience, whereas stress is the psychological and physiological response to an experience (Floyd, 2008). It is important to note that PTS differs from posttraumatic stress disorder (PTSD) in that the former is an official diagnosis given under the strict guidelines of the DSM-5 (APA, 2013), while the latter refers to the normal human response to trauma. Thus, PTSD is the result of long-term PTS.

Organization of the Study

This study flows from the theoretical framework established by a review of the current literature on ethical leadership, moral leadership, trauma, and stress, and 2 Samuel 11:1-27. After a thorough explanation of the methodology, an exhaustive analysis of 2 Samuel 11:1-27 is juxtaposed with the current literature. The findings are then further discussed and summarized along with the implications for current Christian leadership and future empirical research.

2 Samuel 11:1-27 is relevant to the study of ethical leadership because it stands as a pivotal point in the life and leadership of one of history's most storied leaders: King David of Bethlehem, Israel's second king (Finkelstein & Silberman, 2007; Greenberg, 2003). Both the Hebrew and Christian Scriptures identify David as being a "man after God's own heart" (1 Sam 13:14; Acts 13:22, English Standard Version), a "man of war" (1 Sam 16:18), and a man of much bloodshed (1 Chron 28:3). According to Grossman (2009), the prolonged taking of human life through warfare requires a form of *moral distancing* and dehumanizing that allows one to follow through with the most counterhuman act imaginable: killing. Tick (2012) argued that contrary to current trends in psychiatry, the *moral* wounds of warfare have a

greater impact on the life and decision making of a soldier than most admit. Although 2 Samuel 11:1-27 has been studied within the context of sexual sin, narratological ambiguity, and historical succession, no substantial literature has explored the passage through the lens of PTS (Abasili, 2011; Gerhart, 1989; Rosenberg, 1989; Willimon, 1993; Yee, 1988). Ruthven and Ruthven's (2001) exploration of David's life from 2 Samuel 11 to Kings 2 is the closest study to PTS in that it connects David's moral and ethical decline with major depressive disorder (MDD) as defined by the *Diagnostic and Statistical Manual of Mental Disorders* (DSM-5; American Psychiatric Association [APA], 2013).

Although David was a soldier, he was also an executive leader, which almost certainly compounded the level of stress and fatigue in his life as he led the rise of Judah and unification of Israel after the dynasty of Saul (Finkelstein & Silberman, 2007; Greenberg, 2003; Stevens, 2012). In fact, the opening verse of 2 Samuel 11 identifies King David with executive leadership, warfare, decision making, and locus of control: "In the spring of the year, the time when kings go out to battle, David sent Joab, and his servants with him, and all Israel. And they ravaged the Ammonites and besieged Rabbah. But David remained at Jerusalem" (2 Sam 11:1).Because the Bible is appropriate for the study of morality and ethics, the life and leadership of King David as found in 2 Samuel 11:1-27 offers a potential data source for the study of moral and ethical decision making and the presence of stress or fatigue.

King David and 2 Samuel 11:1-27

David of Bethlehem is arguably one of the most influential characters found within the Hebrew Scriptures. It has been often suggested that David was the first *renaissance man* in history, since he successfully functioned as a leader, poet, song writer, warrior, politician, diplomat, and musician (Greenberg, 2003, p. 1). According to traditional interpretations of biblical chronology, David became the King of Judah around 1060 B.C. and the King of unified Israel around 1054 B.C. (Greenberg, 2003). However, according to Greenberg (2003), most scholars have proposed that David's ascendency to the throne happened some 50 years later than the traditional interpretation suggests due to textual "contradictions" (p. 1) and inconsistencies. David's reign stands as the foundation of what many refer to as the Golden age of

Israel's monarchy, which started with King Saul and ended with the reign of David's son: King Solomon (Greenberg, 2003).

Although David is often revered as a hero of the faith and a champion of Israel, Greenberg (2003) suggested that David was not a popular king but instead an ambitious and opportunistic usurper who led a successful rebellion against the house of Saul. According to Greenberg, David's willingness to partner with Israel's enemies in order to fight Saul, the frequency of populist uprisings against David reign, and the Bathsheba/Uriah affair all point to the moral and ethical frailty of David's character and reign. Furthermore, Greenberg argued that a literary–critical analysis of 1 and 2 Samuel and 1 and 2 Chronicles reveals that "much of David's image is mere myth, based on royal propaganda" (p. 15).

For example, although the author of 2 Samuel 11:1-27 presented David's moral and ethical failures in full view, the author of the parallel passage (1 Chron 20:1-3) "omitted the entire scandal from his account" (Greenberg, 2003, p. 149) in order to protect David's image "as a righteous servant" (p. 149). However, the author of 1 Kings 15:4-5 recognized the impact of David's ethical and moral failure so much that even the obituary for David's great-grandson included an account of David's failure:

> "Nevertheless, for David's sake the Lord his God gave him a lamp in Jerusalem, setting up his son after him, and establishing Jerusalem, because David did what was right in the eyes of the Lord and did not turn aside from anything that he commanded him all the days of his life, *except in the matter of Uriah the Hittite* [emphasis added]" (1 Kgs 15:4-5; Greenberg, 2003)

Moreover, Greenberg (2003) suggested that David's remaining in Jerusalem instead of leading the army against the Ammonites as stated in 1 Samuel 11:1 points to the seriousness of David's ethical imperfections. Thus, it appears that a cultural contradiction exists regarding the character of King David as a leader. Therefore, instead of viewing David as *pure hero* or *pure villain*, I use sociorhetorical methodologies to present an accurate and balanced perspective of David's ethical and moral leadership to reconcile the contradictions found in his narrative.

The narrative of David's ascendancy plays an important part in the Hebrew and Christian Scriptures because it links Israel's prophetic past to their Messianic future (Finkelstein & Silberman, 2007). For example, the Hebrew Books of Joshua through 2 Kings are referred to as the Deuteronomist History (DH; Finkelstein & Silberman, 2007). Since these books share linguistic and theological commonality with the Book of Deuteronomy, they offer insight into the applied ethics and morality inherent in the Law of Moses (Finkelstein & Silberman, 2007). In other words, the DH provides readers with a detailed account of how Israel *lived out* the retelling of the Law of Moses as given in the Book of Deuteronomy (Finkelstein & Silberman, 2007).

The narrative of King David as found in 1 and 2 Samuel is central to the DH. Finkelstein and Silberman (2007) stated that David's narrative is a "classic tale of the rise of the young hero, a warrior for the true faith and a man of extraordinary charisma" (p. 7) who takes the place of a failed leader while also wrestling with his own weaknesses. According to Finkelstein and Silberman, the account of David and Bathsheba as told in 2 Samuel 11:1-27 resembles a form of royal life that did not exist until the ninth century B.C. Thus, much of what is known about this period of David's life may have been shaped by those trying to legitimize Solomon's reign or those trying to justify David's unethical behavior in order to present him as God's chosen leader (Finkelstein & Silberman, 2007). Regardless of one's position regarding the historical account of David's failures as seen in 2 Samuel 11:1-27, research has confirmed that David's narrative, failures and all, are central to the Hebrew and Christian Scriptures (Finkelstein & Silberman, 2007; Greenberg, 2003). Given this, I believe that David's failures also offer insight into modern theories relating to ethical and moral failure in leadership.

According to Tick (2012), the savagery of combat damages a critical, yet often overlooked, element of humanity: the soul. As "the center of human consciousness" (Tick, 2012, p. 16), the soul connects to one's belief system, decision-making process, desires and urges, creativity, "intellectual power" (p. 18), volition, sense of love, and sense of *right* and *wrong*. Thus, to wound the soul is to wound the proper function of the aforementioned elements (Tick, 2012). This is especially true as it relates to sexuality and love. Tick suggested that soul trauma in combat compromises normal human sex drives and skews one's perceptions regarding love and intimacy. Moreover, this is due to the fact that "war brings us into the most intense engagement with other human beings" (Tick, 2012, p. 119). Thus, one could argue that as a warrior–king, David dealt with the repercussions of soul trauma.

Tick (2014) argued, "David was even more savage than Saul and committed what we would today consider atrocities" (p. 109). The biblical narrative of David's life mentions multiple occasions of David and his armies attacking and killing men, pillaging cities, wounding animals, and brutally fighting on behalf of God and Israel (Tick, 2014). Tick suggested that David's wartime experiences left him full of pain, darkness, and instability as evidenced by the fluctuating emotional tone found within the Book of Psalms. It is important to note that the first scriptural mention of the Lord *not being pleased* with David does not happen after David's brutality on the battlefield but rather after his sexual immorality, adultery, and treachery as told in 2 Samuel 11:1-27 (Tick, 2014). I seek to improve on Tick's theories by providing a robust exegetical explanation for how David's soul wound connects to leadership fatigue and ethical and moral failure.

Abasili (2011) conducted a narrative analysis of 2 Samuel 11-12 in order to answer the question: Did David rape Bathsheba? According to Abasili, a misunderstanding of the word *rape* has led some to believe that David used his position of power and influence to force Bathsheba into having sexual intercourse. However, this position uses the modern construct of rape, which includes the role of "psychological, emotional, and political coercion" (Abasili, 2011, p. 4) to accomplish sexual conquest, whereas the Hebrew biblical construct of rape always involves the "physical use of power by a man in overpowering a woman into non-consensual sexual intercourse" (p. 6). Even though one cannot argue that David raped Bathsheba in the biblical sense, the evidence is clear that Bathsheba engaged in what she knew was a direct violation of Mosaic law due to David's position as king of Israel (Abasili, 2011). Abasili stated, "David's passion does not permit the enticing of Bathsheba with seductive words; rather he uses his status and authority as a king to get what he wants" (p. 9). Thus, there is no doubt that David, and by default Bathsheba, engaged in unethical and immoral behavior. Although Abasili brought clarity to the nature of David's immorality, it does not thoroughly explain *why* David used his position of power to lay with Bathsheba. Furthermore, Abasili argued that David's decision to stay in Jerusalem is central to the entire 1 Samuel 11-12 narrative. Given this, I seek to answer the *why* question by demonstrating how leadership fatigue impacted David's decision to stay in Jerusalem, which subsequently impacted his behavior toward Bathsheba and Uriah the Hittite.

Willimon (1993) believed that David stayed in Jerusalem for one reason: he was too old to be a hero. Moreover, Willimon suggested that by the time the reader encounters David in 2 Samuel 11:1-27, "King David is at the height of his autonomy and royal power" (p. 222). Thus, it seems that David was used to flexing his *political muscle* in order to meet his personal needs. According to Willimon, David's decisiveness in seeing, sending for, and laying with Bathsheba, along with his elaborate cover-up, demonstrate a connection between sex and politics and sin and narrative. In addition, David's later repentance seems birthed not out of a fundamental understanding of *right* and *wrong* but out of a reminder that "something very intimate" (Willimon, 1993, p. 222) had "been violated" (p. 222) in his narrative-based relationship with God. Thus, one cannot fully understand the sexual sin of David without exploring the story of David.

According to Yee (1988), the Hebrew Scriptures are replete with literary ambiguity. Thus, David's story in 2 Samuel 11:1-27 is open to multiple interpretations, all of which find support within the text (Yee, 1988). Yee suggested that the author of 1 Samuel *sets the stage* for ambiguity by (a) creating various tensions between "character, action, and motive" (p. 241), (b) creating contrast in characters through repeated words and phrases, and (c) fluctuating between narration and dialogue. The problem with this type of ambiguity is it forces upon the reader the burden of interpreting motive (Yee, 1988). This is critical in regards to understanding *why* David stayed in Jerusalem. However, the contrast of characters through repeated words seems to leave clues as to David's motives.

For example, David *sends* for Bathsheba for the purpose of having sex with her, whereas he *sends* for Uriah for the purpose of coaxing him into having sex with her (Yee, 1988). Yee (1988) suggested that the double usage of words such as *wash, lie with/lay with, woman/wife,* and *remain/dwell* subtlety point toward motive without intentionally stating the obvious. Yee argued that the only "unambiguous statement in the narrative is: The thing that David had done displeased the Lord" (p. 244). Thus, the use of literary ambiguity allows the reader to discover truth by *wrestling* with the tensions of the text in the "real world" (Yee, 1988, p. 253). Therefore, the reader is able to make judgements on David's morality by way of basic exegesis as opposed to making judgements because the author has decreed David as moral or immoral (Yee, 1988). I build on Yee's research by avoiding assumptions about David's motives through the use of multilayered hermeneutical methods.

Perhaps one of the most critical elements of this passage is that it provides detail into the first monarchy of Israel (Rosenberg, 1989). According to Rosenberg (1989), the historical portions of the Hebrew Scriptures give more "narrative space" (p. 104) to the life and leadership of David than any other character. Furthermore, in the same way that David is a pivotal character in the history of Israel, his encounter with Bathsheba is a pivotal moment in Israel's history since it serves as a catalyst for the first royal dynasty of Israel (Rosenberg, 1989). Without the David–Bathsheba affair, there is no King Solomon, there is no Rehoboam's folly, and there is no divided kingdom (Rosenberg, 1989). Furthermore, 2 Samuel 11:1 articulates the first time in the Bible that one of Israel's leaders chooses to stay off of the battlefield during a time of war (Rosenberg, 1989). By staying in Jerusalem, David instituted a policy whereby court officials or *agents of the king* began to act on behalf of the monarchy (Rosenberg, 1989). One could argue that this precedent paved the way for Jeroboam, a court official, to later challenge the house of David, thus dividing the kingdom (1 Kgs 11:26-27). Given the significance of 2 Samuel 11:1-27 on the political history of Israel, I also build on Rosenberg's work by exploring the ethical and moral ramifications of David's behavior as seen in the passage.

Kings played an important leadership role in the Ancient Near East (ANE). Stevens (2012) posited that kings were chosen in the ANE by one of four methods: (a) popular demand due to proven competence, (b) genealogical precedence, (c) use of force/coup, or (d) imposition by a foreign entity. According to Stevens, although "kingship was the virtually universal method of governance" ("God as King," para. 1) in the ANE, the God of Israel never intended for His people to any other ruler than Him. Thus, as king, David was expected by God to govern according to the will and character of the Divine King (Stevens, 2012, loc. 366). However, David's actions in 2 Samuel 11:1-27 are contradictory to his last words, which "acknowledge the efficacy of ruling with justice derived from God" (Stevens, 2012, "Securing the Property," para. 4). In spite of the biblical declaration that God was not pleased with David's affair with Bathsheba, David is disqualified from building the temple of God due to his warfare and not his sexual immorality (Stevens, 2012). Almost ironically, Solomon is chosen to build the temple of God because he was a man of peace, yet Solomon exponentially failed in the area of sexual immorality (Stevens, 2012). Furthermore, David's affair with Bathsheba set the stage for a succession struggle between David's sons, Adonijah and Solomon, which finds replication in the later struggle between Rehoboam and Jeroboam (Stevens, 2012). Given this, it is critical to explore how David's ethical and moral leadership as seen in 2 Samuel 11:1-27 may have shaped the ethics of future leaders in Israel.

It is important to note that several prominent women also play a key role in the succession narrative of Israel: Tamar, Ruth, and Bathsheba (Berger, 2009). One could argue that the primary purposes of the Book of Ruth is to introduce the character of David into the sacred text. According to Berger (2009), the author of Ruth "sought to provide a portrait of the Davidic ancestry that would offset any unfavorable associations generated by the morally suspect encounter between Judah and Tamar that produced the royal bloodline" (p. 435). Berger suggested that the *tragic flaw* of David's behavior in 2 Samuel 11 is that he did not model the empathy of Boaz in his treatment of Bathsheba and Uriah. In fact, David modeled a lack of empathy as displayed in Judah's treatment of Tamar (Gen 38:1-24). Berger believed that the author of the Book of Ruth was shaped by the Judah and Tamar narrative and the David and Bathsheba affair. Thus, in order to clean up the presentation of the royal Davidic bloodline, the author presented Ruth and Boaz as *better story* in order to show that David was not destined for moral failure (Berger, 2009). The use of sociorhetorical intertexture analysis in this book allows us to further explore Berger's theories in view of leadership fatigue and ethical and moral leadership.

King David is a central figure in the Hebrew and Christian Scriptures. Yet, in spite of the fact that his greatest moral failure is central to the history of ancient Israel, very little research explores the underlying factors behind that failure. If David was *a man after God's own heart*, then it is important to understand how this man eventually acted in a way that runs contrary to the character of God as revealed in the Hebrew Scriptures (1 Sam 13:14; Acts 13:22). Therefore, this book presents David as a *case* for how leadership fatigue influences ethical and moral decision making and behavior.

The story of King David's affair with Bathsheba and his part in the murder of Uriah the Hittite is found within a much larger portion of the Hebrew Scriptures known as the Deuteronomist History (DH). Scholars have been at odds as to the primary author of the DH since this portion the Hebrew Scriptures covers a large period in the history of Israel. However, the consensus agrees that whether pre-exilic or postexilic, the DH as represented in the modern Bible is likely a revised version of an earlier document (Campbell & O'Brien, 2000). Furthermore, it is widely accepted that the DH was informed by several critical documents: (a) the Yahwistic narratives or J, (b) the Priestly narratives or P, and the Elohist narratives or E (Peckham, 1985). According to Peckham (1985), J is a foundational literary source for the DH, P is an interpretive supplement to the earliest versions of the DH, and E is a further variant that supplements J, P, and the DH. As for *who* actually wrote or revised portions of the DH, some have argued for the prophet Nathan or a pre-exilic author during the reign and reforms of King Josiah (Campbell & O'Brien, 2000). However, the strongest evidence suggests that the priestly line of Anathoth—of which belonged Abiathar (David's high priest) and the prophet Jeremiah—compiled and revised the documents that would eventually become the Book of Judges through 2 Kings (Peterson, 2014).

Martin Noth's seminal 1943 work titled *Historical Studies* is widely recognized as the first exhaustive treatment of the DH (Campbell & O'Brien, 2000). Noth's (1981) original hypothesis argues that the DH represents a single literary unity arranged by an individual editor or closely related editors whose work was influenced by the theology and language of the Book of Deuteronomy. Noth suggested that the DH was informed by a wide variety of extant sources, which may explain why some scholars have viewed 1 and 2 Samuel as an apology for the life and leadership of King David (Berger, 2009; Peterson, 2014). Moreover, Noth argued that the entire historical tradition of the Hebrew Scriptures "is contained within a few large compilations" (p. 1): The Pentateuch, the Deuteronomist (Dtr), and the Chronicler. According to Noth (1958), the author of the DH "passed on numerous sources from different periods . . . partly *in extenso*, partly in extracts" (p. 42), which "conveyed to posterity a mass of valuable traditional material" (p. 42) that laid the groundwork for future Israelite historians. Noth contended that without the work of the author of the DH, much of what is known about Deuteronomy, Joshua, Judges, Samuel, and Kings would have been lost forever. Peckham (1985) argued that while brilliant, Noth's theory is based on weak literary and historical assumptions. However, when one considers the "complete and coherent" (Peckham, 1985, p. 7) nature of the DH, its distinct syntax, narrative progression and episodes, it is evident that Noth's original theory is "substantially correct" (p. 73).

According to Römer (2007), it seems probable that Noth's (1981) personal context as a scholar stuck in a war-torn and morally bankrupt nation, such as Nazi Germany, may have influenced his understanding of the DH. Regardless of how one views Noth's theories on the DH, most scholars have agreed that his work plays a pivotal role in understanding how the history of Israel was saved from total loss (Peckham, 1985; Peterson, 2014; Römer, 2007). Some have suggested that the DH was edited during and after the reforms of King Josiah (Dtr[1]), while others have suggested that the DH was primarily compiled and edited in an exilic context (Nelson-Jones, 1981; Peterson, 2014). The latter hypothesis is referred to as the exilic Deuteronomist (Dtr[2]). Nevertheless, the DH's connection with God's moral law as seen in Deuteronomy with the failed experiment known as the *Israelite Monarchy* has several implications for the current study's examination of ethical and moral leadership (Campbell & O'Brien, 2000; Peterson, 2014; Rae, 2009).

As for the authorship of 1 and 2 Samuel, scholars traditionally have presented Samuel, Nathan, Gad, Hushai, and even King David as having contributed material to this collective volume on the early days Israel's monarchy (Peterson, 2014). However, a recent theory suggests that Jeremiah is responsible for combining this material into one body of work (Peterson, 2014). Furthermore, since 2 Samuel presents King David as the antithesis of King Saul, it is believed that the author of 2 Samuel had a close relationship with David (Campbell & O'Brien, 2000; Peterson, 2014). Peterson (2014) posited that since Nathan, Solomon, and Bathsheba are not presented in the most favorable light in the succession narratives, it is more than likely that 2 Samuel is Abiathar's way of presenting David as the *right* type of king and himself as being on the *right* side of history when compared to the Prophet Nathan and King Solomon (1 Kgs 1:11-14). Furthermore, Abiathar more than likely recorded the history of David in 1 and 2 Samuel as a way of distancing himself from the house of Eli and the reign of Solomon, since

Solomon banished him due to Abiathar's siding with David's fourth son Adonijah during the succession dispute (1 Kgs 2:26-27).

As David's high priest, Abiathar would have had great concern over the ethical and moral condition of Israel's king. Thus, if Abiathar was the author of 2 Samuel, it makes sense that he would not want to side with the son of Bathsheba when it came the royal succession after David's death, since Bathsheba and Solomon are the result of David's greatest moral failure. Peterson (2014) also connected Abiathar with the authorship of the Book of Judges, which contains "explicit connections" ("The Succession Narrative," para. 6) with 2 Samuel. Since the role of the priesthood in ancient Israel was to preserve and teach the law, which implies a high degree of literacy and scholarship, it is not unreasonable to consider Abiathar and Jeremiah as being contributors to what would become 1 and 2 Samuel, especially since both had connections to the priestly line of Anathoth thus confirming the DH theories regarding closely related editors (Noth, 1981, 1987; Peterson, 2014).

For example, Jeremiah stayed in Jerusalem after its destruction by the Babylonians; his own writings give evidence that he had time to record the supposed final days of Israel's history during this period, and the introduction to his book connects him with the priestly line of Anathoth, to whom also belonged Abiathar (Jer 1:1, 39:14, 40:6, 41:1; Peterson, 2014). Furthermore, the multiple redactions of Noth's (1981) theory reveal a gap in the literature regarding the authorship of the DH, thus allowing room for theories relating to Abiathar and Jeremiah as playing a critical role in the final version of the DH (Nelson-Jones, 1981; Peterson, 2014; Peckham, 1985; Römer, 2007; Ross, 2015).

Given this, I approach 2 Samuel 11:1-27 with an understanding that the author was Abiathar and the compiler was Jeremiah, the former of whom was personally invested in the life of David and both of whom served as stewards of the moral values of God (Peterson, 2014; Ross, 2015). I also place the date of the writing of 2 Samuel between 1010 B.C and 950 B.C. or during the reign of David and briefly during the reign of King Solomon (Finkelstein & Silberman, 2007; Peterson, 2014). Finally, use the conceptual framework of 2 Samuel being part of the Dtr^2, with Jeremiah as the compiler and minor editor (Noth, 1981; Peterson, 2014). Thus, it is likely that the original audience of 2 Samuel consisted of exilic and postexilic Israelites, many of whom were learning about their nation's history for the first time. Based upon the preceding discussion, my research is conducted based on the assumption that Abiathar authored and Jeremiah compiled and edited 2 Samuel to warn Israel about the consequences of violating the moral law of God and to present an apology for King David as being God's ideal leader as opposed to King Saul or King Solomon.

Scholars have claimed that 2 Samuel 11 follows the systematic and *character-centric* organizational patterns found within the first eight books of the Bible (Noth, 1981; Peckham, 1985; Römer, 2007). Specifically, 2 Samuel uses historical storytelling to advance the narrative of Israel from its formative years in the desert of Sinai toward its golden age during the unified kingdom under David's leadership (Noth, 1981, 1987; Peckham, 1985; Römer, 2007). Some have suggested that the structure of 1 and 2 Samuel serves as both an apologetic for the leadership of David and an indictment on Israel's rejection of the theocracy (Finkelstein & Silberman, 2007; Peterson, 2014). However, 2 Samuel deviates from the normal form of biblical narration in that it presents the historical chain of events surrounding David, Bathsheba, Joab, and Uriah in a neutral manner as opposed to assigning the moralistic epithets that are commonplace throughout the Hebrew Scriptures (Sternberg, 1987). Thus, both Campbell (2007) and Yee (1988) argued that the story of David and Bathsheba found within 2 Samuel 11:1-27 is one of the most ambiguous narratives within the Hebrew Scriptures.

For example, the odd inclusion of what appears to be a benign report of a military campaign rapidly transitions without warning into a narrative of "sexual wrongdoing, deceit, murder" (Campbell, 2007, "Chapter 6 Discussion," para. 1), pregnancy, and marriage. Notwithstanding, Noth (1981) argued that the DH is "extremely interested in chronological data" (p. 18). According to Noth, the original author of the DH assumes that there are no gaps in its chronology. Thus, one could argue that the structure of 2 Samuel 11 uses chronology to resolve the apparent ambiguity found within the passage. Furthermore, the chronology of 2 Samuel 11 is a microcosm of the macronarrative of succession found within 2 Samuel 9 through 2 Kings 2 (Berger, 2009; Noth, 1981; Peterson, 2014; Stevens, 2012).

Campbell (2007) suggested that 2 Samuel 11:1-27 falls within a larger framework, which also includes 2 Samuel 12:1-31. According to Campbell's outline of 2 Samuel 11, the passage consists of three sections: (a) the opening

(Rabbah besieged), (b) story of David and Bathsheba, and (c) the resolution of the Bathsheba and Uriah complication. Within Campbell's outline are subsections dealing with David's interest in Bathsheba, their intercourse, and David's dealing with Uriah the Hittite. However, Campbell posited, "To name the major moments inevitably means bypassing much of the detail" "Chapter 6 Discussion," para. 2), whereas naming the detail "inevitably leads to baffling complexity and boredom" "Chapter 6 Discussion," para. 2). Youngblood (1992) argued for a chiastic outline of 2 Samuel 11-12 that blends that chronology of the narrative with a specific thematic pattern that sandwiches David's moral and ethical failure between two descriptions of battle.

A. David sends Joab to seige Rabbah (11:1)

B. David sleeps with Bathsheba/Bathsheba pregnant (11:2-5)

C. David has Uriah Killed (11:6-17)

D. Joab sends David a message (11:18-27a)

E. The Lord is angry with David (11:27b)

D. The Lord sends David a message (12:1-14)

C. The Lord allows David's son to die (12:15-23)

B. David sleeps with Bathsheba/Bathsheba pregnant (12:24-25)

A. Joab sends for David to seige Rabbah (12:26-31)

Figure 1: Chiastic outline of 2 Samuel 11-12. Adapted from *1 and 2 Samuel: Expositor's Bible Commentary*, by R. F. Youngblood, 1992, Grand Rapids, MI: Zondervan. Copyright 1992 by R. F. Youngblood.

Since the focus of this book is to explore the impact of leadership fatigue on ethical and moral decision making, and since the context of 2 Samuel 11 implies the presence of stress and trauma in King David's life, and since the use of chronology in the passage serves to advance the storyline and uncover meaning, I also approach 2 Samuel 11 in chronological order. Given this, I divide 2 Samuel 11 into five sections. The introduction and conclusion sections focus on the historical and relational contexts of the narrative, whereas the remaining three sections center on David's leadership and moral and ethical interactions with others.

Table 1: Five Sections of 2 Samuel 11:1-27

Section	Focus	Verses
1	Introduction—The siege of Rabbah	2 Samuel 11:1
2	David and Bathsheba—Arousal and affair	2 Samuel 11:2-5
3	David and Uriah—Attempted conspiracy	2 Samuel 11:6-13
4	David and Joab—Conspiracy and murder	2 Samuel 11:14-25
5	Conclusion—David marries Bathsheba	2 Samuel 11:26-27

The current study involves an in-depth interdisciplinary exploration of 2 Samuel 11:1-27 and centers on three principles: (a) hermeneutics is a logical and orderly science, (b) hermeneutics demands the artful use of imagination, and (c) hermeneutics is a pneumatalogical spiritual act (Osborne, 2006). Furthermore, since "meaning is not prior to, but a product of the reader's activity" (Vanhoozer, 2009, p. 23), the current researcher approached the Hebrew and Christian Scriptures with a hermeneutic of humility that identifies the Scriptures as being a divinely inspired and authoritative source of data wherein belief leads to understanding. However, it is important to note that these beliefs "do not always parallel the practices, ideologies, and institutions" found in the Ancient Near East (ANE; Merrill et al., 2011, "The Gap Between," para. 2). Since the current study centers on a historical narrative, it was important to examine the historical and cultural world of 2 Samuel 11:1-27 along with the use of language in the pericope with an understanding that the current study's presuppositions regarding the divine origins of morality are not dependent on ANE ideology (Merrill et al., 2011). The primary objective of the current interdisciplinary study is to examine the role of leadership fatigue and trauma in ethical and moral decision making as seen in 2 Samuel 11:1-27. The study uses sociorhetorical analysis to explore the presence of stress, trauma, and burnout in the life of King David as well as the leadership behaviors and decisions exhibited by King David in the aforementioned pericope. The study examines 2 Samuel 11:1-27 through the English Standard Version, which primarily interprets the Hebrew Scriptures from the Masoretic text as found in the Biblia Hebraica Stuttgartensia ("Translation Philosophy," 2015). Other translations are consulted as needed. The study also uses the English Standard Version's

Strong's concordance reference list to access key Hebrew root words during various phases of analysis. The rigor of sociorhetorical analysis, the validity of exegetical methodologies as seen previous leadership research, and the recognition of the researcher's theological and philosophical perspectives should result in the extraction of objective data from 2 Samuel 11:1-27.

According to Burns (1978), "The crisis of leadership today is the mediocrity or irresponsibility of so many of the men and women and power, but leadership rarely rises to the full need of it" (p. 3). However, one could argue that although it may be irresponsible to not take leadership seriously, it is equally irresponsible to not search for solutions to leadership failures. This study seeks to take responsibility for the current leadership crisis by filling a critical gap in the literature concerning ethical and moral leadership. Crowther (2012a) argued that the embracing of theology through sociorhetorical methodologies not only addresses the spiritual and ontological elements of leadership, it demonstrates that unique biblical models of leadership parallel contemporary models of leadership. Henson (2015) further developed the aforementioned construct by proving that secular and Christian leadership are the result of a false dichotomy that flows from a lack of understanding regarding universal moral values. The current study seeks to further explore how the Hebrew and Christian Scriptures offer insight into organizational leadership. Specifically, this study seeks to be one of the few within the field of organizational leadership to use sociorhetorical methodologies within the context of the Hebrew Scriptures and ethical and moral leadership. The results of this study should not only further validate sociorhetorical analysis methodologies, they should also advance the literature regarding ethical and moral decision making and behavior. Now, let us jump into the *meat* of the narrative. In the next five chapters we will walk through 2 Samuel 11, with sociorhetorical analysis as our guide.

CHAPTER 6

David Stays Put - 2 Samuel 11:1

2 Samuel 11:1 - Why Did David Stay in Jerusalem?

There are progressive and sensory–aesthetic inner textual layers to consider in the first section of 2 Samuel 11, even though the section only consists of one verse: "In the spring of the year, the time when kings go out to battle, David sent Joab, and his servants with him, and all Israel. And they ravaged the Ammonites and besieged Rabbah. But David remained at Jerusalem" (2 Sam 11:1). Robbins (1996a) argued that sensory–aesthetic texture is often designed to appeal to certain emotions while calling attention to certain *tones*. This section opens by placing the narrative in the spring time. In Ancient Near East (ANE) culture, wars were typically fought when the weather permitted the ease of travel and favorable conditions for the static nature of massive warfare (Baldwin, 2008). Evidence also suggests that the Israelite army typically went out to war during the spring since this would free the able-bodied men to work at home during the autumn harvest (Gordon, 1999). Furthermore, spring time was the ideal time for warfare since "the enemy's wheat fields were full of ripe grain" (Andrews & Bergen, 2009, p. 271).

Thus, Section 1 appeals to the basic Hebrew understanding of leadership behavior. According to Campbell (2005), the Masoretic text uses the word *hammal'kim* (messengers) instead of *hammelakim* (kings) to describe those who went out to war during the spring time. However, since "messengers are sent" and "only kings go out" (Campbell, 2005, "Chapter 6 Textual Issues," para. 2), it is clear that the word *kings* accurately represented those who went out to war in the spring time. As noted in the chiastic outline of 2 Samuel 11-12, *messengers* and messages play a critical role in the development of the narrative, which may explain why the author chose to use a play on words in the first verse.

Verse 1 also establishes a repetitive and progressive pattern involving the *sent* motif (Baldwin, 2008; Sternberg, 1987). During the time when kings, specifically David, should have been at war, David chose to remain in Jerusalem and instead *sent* Joab and the Israelite army to battle at Rabbah. According to Youngblood (1992), this language is designed to paint David in stark contrast to the able-bodied men of Israel by demonstrating how one wrong decision can escalate into a series of terrible and sinful decisions. Although it was not David's common practice to stay home while his men went to war, the language of verse 1 sets the tone for the rest of the passage by demonstrating the fact that David had the power to come and go and to *send* and receive as he saw fit (Youngblood, 1992).

There are also several social intertextures and social and cultural textures relating to roles, norms, and power to consider in this brief section. As mentioned, David stayed in Jerusalem when the cultural norm demanded that kings go off to war with their men (Gordon, 1999; Sternberg, 1987). Thus, David's behavior would have been considered countercultural to the original audience of 2 Samuel. In fact, Campbell (2005) indicated, "The difference between the words for messengers and kings in Hebrew is one consonant, one aleph" ("Chapter 6 Discussion," para. 4). Campbell argued that this intentionally ambiguous language emphasizes the importance of *messengers* within the narrative while also highlighting David's dependence upon those under his care. However, Gordon (1999) suggested that the Masoretic text uses the word *messengers* instead of *kings* in verse 1 as a "scribal attempt to shade off the irony" (p. 252) of David *sending* others to do his duties. Moreover, this subtle play on words is likely an attempt by Abiathar to redeem David's reputation in view of his immoral and unethical behavior that begins immediately in the second section of the passage.

In summary, there are multiple issues relating to leadership in the opening section of this passage, which set the tone for the remaining sections. First, King David abdicated his primary responsibility as Israel's commander in chief by choosing to remain in Jerusalem during the optimum fighting season. This behavior is so abnormal given David's history that one is left to assume that something, whether internal or external, changed in the character of David between the battle of Halem (2 Samuel 10:15-19) and the siege of Rabbah. Second, David's *sending* of Joab, the servants, and all of Israel into battle indicates a shift from the altruism, service, and vision found within David's earliest manifestations of leadership and toward a Saul-esque detachment from responsibility (Serrano, 2014). Finally, whereas David was accustomed to "great personal risk" (Serrano, 2014, p. 39) in battle, the opening section of the passage places David in the position of self-preservation and self-centeredness, both of which indicate a lack of health in David's leadership.

CHAPTER 7

David Gets Bathsheba - 2 Samuel 11:2-5

2 Samuel 11:2-5

Section 2 contains inner textual, social and cultural textual, and sacred textual layers, all of which offer insight into David's ethical and moral leadership. In verses 2-4, the author shifted the narrative away from the Ammonite war toward David's behavior in Jerusalem. The sensory–aesthetic texture of the second section places the passage in the latter portion of the day (2 Sam 11:2). Some have suggested that David arose from an afternoon nap and restlessly paced on the roof, as evidenced by the Hebrew verb form used in verse 2 (Baldwin, 2008; Sternberg, 1987). Others have claimed that David "got up from his bed" (Andrews & Bergen, 2009, p. 271) during the evening since the Hebrew word *ereb*, which is used in the Masoretic text, has a literal translation of dusk, evening, or night (Youngblood, 1992). Whether in the afternoon or evening, the one thing that is certain is that David got out of bed and walked aimlessly on the roof of the palace. The double mention of the word *roof* (2 Sam 11:2) not only provides the reader with a spatial point of reference for David's wandering, it also reminds the reader of David's elevated status over all of his domain (Baldwin, 2008). Again, as with Section 1, social norms and cultural concepts of power are interwoven in Section 2 to paint a contrast between the expected behavior of the king and David's lived-out behavior within the passage.

Rooftops in the ANE were usually flat and functioned much like modern-day backyard decks (Andrews & Bergen, 2008). Furthermore, these spaces were often a place of refuge on warm evenings or during times of stress as evidenced in 1 Samuel 9:25 (Andrews & Bergen, 2008). Therefore, it is safe to assume that when David *sees* Bathsheba bathing on the roof (2 Sam. 11:2), he is already in an emotive state that does not reflect calm, balance, or a godly disposition. According to Baldwin (2008), the Hebrew idiom translated "very beautiful" (loc. 3785) means that Bathsheba was so beautiful that David's glance quickly became a gaze. Youngblood (1992) argued that the term *very beautiful* is the same term used to describe Rebekah (Gen 24:16), Vashti (Esth 1:11), Esther (Esth 2:7), and David himself (1 Sam 16:12). Moreover, since the Law of Moses required that Israelite women wash after their monthly time of impurity (Lev 15:13-19), it is also safe to assume that Bathsheba was probably engaging in a ritual cleaning at the end of her menstrual cycle (Andrews & Bergen, 2008). This is supported by the latter mentioning of Bathsheba "purifying herself from her uncleanness" (2 Sam 11:4). Verse 4 does not read *she purified herself* but, rather, *she was purifying herself*, which indicates that Abiathar wanted the original audience to know two things: Bathsheba was living within the moral commands of God, and David was the only one who could have fathered Bathsheba's child (Sternberg, 1987).

Upon seeing Bathsheba, David sent a messenger to inquire about her (v. 3). The unnamed messenger's response connects to social and cultural roles as well as ANE norms relating to community, family, and the moral commands of God. Although David seems set on treating Bathsheba like an object, the messenger placed Bathsheba within the context of humanity: "Is not this Bathsheba, the daughter of Eliam, the wife of Uriah the Hittite?" (v. 3). Bathsheba was not just some random woman bathing on a rooftop. Her husband, Uriah, was one of David's foreign mercenary warriors and officers known as the *mighty men* (Na'aman, 1988). According to Hauer (1978), "The chief instrument of David's military accomplishments was a relatively small, mobile and tough force of professional heavy infantry" (p. 68). As illustrated in Table 2, the *mighty men* played an important role in Israel's military campaigns during David's reign. Based on the typical pattern of warfare in the ANE, it is safe to assume that even if the Scriptures do not explicitly identify the mighty men as being present, they were more than likely involved in all of David's military campaigns. Scholars have presented *mighty men* as a blanket term for David's elite mercenary forces, which includes subgroups such as the Thirty, the Three, the Cherethites, the Pelethites, and the Gittites (Hauer, 1978; Na'aman, 1988; Youngblood, 1992).

Table 2: David's Campaigns and the Mighty Men

Campaign	Field force	Reference
War with the house of Saul	Professional army of Judah	2 Sam 2:11-4:12
The Battle for Jerusalem	All of Israel (professionals and militia)	2 Sam 5:6-10; 1 Chron 11:4-9
Rephaim Campaign and War with the Philistines	Professional army	2 Sam 5:17-25, 23:13-17
War with the Philistines, various campaigns	Professional army, the men of Israel (militia)	2 Sam 21:15-22, 23:9-10
War with Moab	N/A	2 Sam 8:2-3
War with Ammonites (Phase 1)	The Mighty Men	2 Sam 10:6-14
War with Arameans (Phase 1)	All of Israel (professionals and militia)	2 Sam 10:15-19
War with Ammonites (Phase 2)	All of Israel (professionals and militia)	2 Sam 11:1-12:31
War with Arameans (Phase 2)	N/A	2 Sam 8:3-8
War with Edomites	All of Israel under (professionals and militia)	2 Sam 8:13-14; 1 Chron 18:12-13; 1 Kgs 11:14-17
War with Absalom	The Mighty Men	2 Sam 15:7-19:43
War with Sheba	The Mighty Men	2 Sam 20:1-22
Solomon's ascendency	Cherethites and Pelethites	1 Kgs 1:1-53

Note. Adapted from "David's army," by C. E. Hauer, 1978, *Concordia Journal,* 4(2), 68-72. Copyright 1978 by C. E. Hauer.

According to the Hebrew Scriptures, Uriah the Hittite was a member of David's elite officer corps known as the Thirty (2 Sam 23:34). As a member

72 CARLO A. SERRANO, PH.D.

of the Thirty, Uriah functioned as one of David's trusted bodyguards and most loyal warriors (Hauer, 1978). Figure 2 illustrates Uriah's proximity to the king according to the Israelite chain of command during David's reign. Bathsheba's father, Eliam, was also one of David's mighty men and a member of the Thirty, which means that David had more than one relational connection to Bathsheba (2 Sam 23:34; Youngblood, 1992). Furthermore, Eliam was the son of Ahithopel, who served as David's counselor (2 Sam 15:12). Therefore, Bathsheba was an upper-class woman with connections to the king through her husband, father-in-law, and grandfather-in-law (Youngblood, 1992).

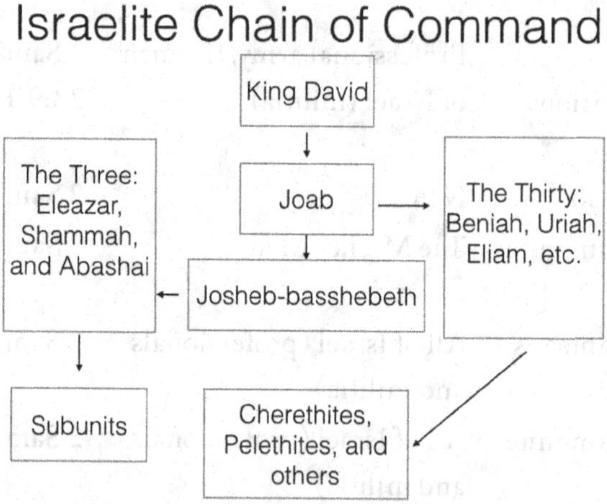

Israelite Chain of Command

King David

The Three: Eleazar, Shammah, and Abashai

Joab

The Thirty: Beniah, Uriah, Eliam, etc.

Josheb-basshebeth

Subunits

Cherethites, Pelethites, and others

Figure 2: Israelite chain of command based on 2 Samuel 23:8-39.

Even though it was immediately brought to David's attention that Bathsheba was not only the wife of another man, she was the wife of one of his most trusted and elite warriors, David ignored the moral commands of God and the societal norms of Israel, sent for Bathsheba, had intercourse with her, and then sent her home (Andrews & Bergen, 2008; Sternberg, 1987; 2 Sam 11:4). It is important to note the author's use of perspective in the narrative, especially in regards to David's conversation with the messenger known as *one* (2 Sam 11: 3). Hertzberg (1965) suggested that David inquired as to Bathsheba's identity because he could only see her silhouetted figure from his rooftop vantage point. Thus, from David's initial perspective, she was just a naked woman on a rooftop. However, the inclusion of the messenger's detailed description of Bathsheba's true identity shifts the perspective away from David and toward God's. One could argue that the voice of the messenger in verse 3 is the voice of the Lord trying to talk some sense back into David. Furthermore, in spite of Bathsheba's silence in the first four verses of Section 1, the narrative is incomplete without an understanding of her perspective.

Although the author did not specify a length of time between verses 4 and 5, the text clearly points to a time frame of no more than 2 months. This is evidenced by the fact that Bathsheba sent a messenger to alert David of her pregnant state (2 Sam 11:5). Since Bathsheba was obviously known in the community (2 Sam 11:3), and since the Law of Moses demanded a death sentence for adultery (Lev 20:10; Deut 22:22), it seems logical that Bathsheba would want to alert the king of her pregnancy immediately since David was the only one in the land who had the power to save her life. Thus, one finds three competing ethical perspectives in Section 1: (a) David—heart set on self-gratification, (b) the messenger—the voice of reason, and (c) Bathsheba—heart set on obedience to God and submission to the king. The inner texture of the second section of contains several repetitive–progressive and sensory–aesthetic textures, all of which confirm the escalation of David's immoral and unethical behavior.

Table 3: Inner Texture of 2 Samuel 11:2-5

Verse	Repetitive texture	Opening–Middle–Closing	Progressive texture
2	David, his, roof (2x), he, woman (2x)	11:2 It happened, late one afternoon	David, arose, walking, saw
3	David, one/ messenger	11:3-4 And David sent and inquired about the woman ... David sent messengers and took her	David, sent, inquired, took, lay with, she returned
4	David, her, woman, messengers		
5	David, woman, she, sent/ messengers	11:5 And the woman conceived, and she sent and told David, "I am pregnant."	Woman, conceived, sent

Section 2 ends with a blunt statement from Bathsheba regarding the initial aftermath of David's behavior: "I am pregnant" (2 Sam 11:5b). Scholars have been at odds as to Bathsheba's complicity in the affair. Some have argued that Bathsheba had no choice but to submit to the will of the king, while others have suggested that Bathsheba more than likely agreed to David's plan of action following the unplanned pregnancy (Abasili, 2011; Gordon, 1999). Nevertheless, Abiathar presents the facts of the affair in a rapid "assembly line fashion" (Sternberg, 1987, p. 197)—not to emphasize the minor details but to display the steady escalation of David's immoral behavior. Herein lies another contrast between Bathsheba and David. Uriah the Hittite was a foreign mercenary as evidenced by the fact that the author almost always used *Hittite* to identify Uriah throughout the narrative (Gordon, 1999). The Hittites mentioned in the Hebrew Scriptures were a people group that lived in Northern Palestine during the Late Bronze Age (Collins, 2007). The Hittites, along with the Jebusites, Amorites, and Hivites, are represented in Scripture as a type of "counteridentity" (Collins, 2007, p. 209) to the people of Israel.

Scholars have agreed that it was commonplace for ex-patriots to join King David's army, a notion that finds substantiation in the list of David's mighty men (Kim, 2002). Two of David's chief officers, Ahimelech and Uriah, were Hittites (Collins, 2007). Also, the last seven names mentioned in the list of David's mighty men are all non-Israelite foreigners (Kim, 2002). From a sociocultural perspective, these foreign officers represent a culture of integration that one could argue runs contrary to God's commands regarding Israelite isolation and cultural purity (Deut 7:1-6). The eventual demise of the United Israelite Kingdom under Solomon's reign is in many ways connected to foreign alliances, diplomatic marriages, and the Hittites (Collins, 2007).

Moreover, Bathsheba, the mother of Solomon is listed amongst the Gentile ancestress of Jesus in Matthew 1:3-6, which implies that she too was of non-Israelite ancestry (Youngblood, 1999). Thus, it is safe to assume that Bathsheba was a convert to Judaism, which connects to the sacred texture of the passage. This makes the contrast between her adherence to the law more striking when compared to the king of Israel's posture toward the moral commands of God. It also further amplifies the ironic nature of Uriah the Hittite's high moral posture in comparison to King David's immoral behavior.

For example, Section 1 mentions Bathsheba's purification ritual to compare her adherence to the Mosaic law with David's disobedience to the moral commands of God. This type of comparison between characters continues throughout the entire passage. Furthermore, the ending of Section 2 fills the ambiguous gaps left by the author in the earlier portions of the section by leaving no room for misunderstanding regarding David's intentional and immoral behavior (Sternberg, 1987). Therefore, although Section 1 starts off with a seemingly innocuous statement regarding the political affairs of Israel and Section 2 begins with a commentary on David's postnap activities, Section 2 ends with a clear picture of a moral and ethical dilemma in need of a solution.

In summary, Section 2 illustrates how David's abdication of leadership responsibility placed him in a position to make a series of unethical and immoral decisions. This is not to say that David's remaining in Jerusalem caused his adultery. However, it is obvious that, if David had been present for the siege of Rabbah with Joab, he would not have seen Bathsheba bathing on the rooftop. David's quick and methodical action in *sending* for Bathsheba, his sexual immorality, and ambivalence to the commands of God provide an answer for the inherent gap left in Section 1. Up until this point in the narrative of David Son of Jesse and King of Israel, there is nothing in the text to indicate a wavering in his faith or a gap in his morality. However, what is consistent in the narrative of David is the evidence that suggests he had been in a *war footing* for 24 years, half of which took place while he was ruling all of Israel as its chief executive and commander in chief (Reese, 1994). Therefore, it is safe to assume that David stayed in Jerusalem because his moral foundation was compromised due to the stress and pressure of leadership and the trauma of war, both of which produced unethical and immoral behavior.

CHAPTER 8

David Gets Crafty - 2 Samuel 11:6-13

2 Samuel 11:6-13

Section 3 contains inner textual, social and cultural textual, and sacred textual layers along with subtle intertexture and ideological textures. These textures further substantiate David's compromised morality. In verses 6-13, the author presents a blunt account of David's response to Bathsheba's pregnancy. According to Hertzberg (1965), "As in Israel, even the king does not stand *extra legem*" (p. 319): As the King of Israel, David would have been familiar with God's divine policies toward sexual immorality (Deut 22:22). Since David was not above the law, and since the king represented the highest authority in Israel, one could argue that David's decision-making process in Section 2 was based on a desire to save Israel and the name of the Lord from shame. Thus, David's subsequent response to Bathsheba's pregnancy flowed from his knowledge of the Mosaic law, a desire to protect Israel, and self-preservation.

The sensory–aesthetic texture of Section 2 compares David's internal conflict with the external conflict between Israel and the Ammonites. Furthermore, this conflict is manifested in Uriah's rejection of comfort. In verse 6, Uriah was summoned back to Jerusalem, and after some brief small talk regarding the minutiae of the siege of Rabbah (2 Sam 11:7), David presented Uriah with the comforts of a bath and royal gifts (2 Sam 11:8), the comfort of home and the benefits of the marriage bed (2 Sam 11:9-11), and the power of strong drink (2 Sam 11:13). Instead of giving into the natural desires of the flesh, Uriah appeared to have taken the moral high ground. As an executive officer in Israel's army and as a fierce warrior, it is safe to assume that Uriah longed for rest, strong drink, good food, and his wife. However, unlike David who gave in to temptation regarding Bathsheba, Uriah resisted the temptation to find comfort at home and instead chose to take the posture of a servant (2 Sam 11:9,13).

Sternberg (1987) proposed three possible hypotheses regarding Uriah's foreknowledge of David's immoral behavior. Hypothesis one argues that David sent for Uriah because David believed that Uriah was ignorant of the affair (Sternberg, 1987). According to Sternberg, "The strongest argument for the hypothesis that David thinks Uriah is ignorant is the sending of the letter by hand" (p. 209), which implies that no one other than David, Bathsheba, and the messengers knew about the affair. Hypothesis two argues that David believed that Uriah was fully aware of the affair (Sternberg, 1987). The strongest argument for this hypothesis is the irrational nature of David's subsequent behavior as illustrated in Section 3 of the passage. Simply put, "David cannot have been in his right mind" (Sternberg, 1987, p. 211) when he ordered the murder of one of his closest officers and strongest leaders. Hypothesis three finds the most support in the text and in the literature: Both David and the reader are uncertain as to Uriah's knowledge of the affair (Campbell, 2005; Sternberg, 1987). Although the inner texture of Section 3 does not answer the questions relating to Uriah's knowledge of David's affair, it does demonstrate the rapid progression of David's unethical decision making and his exploitation of others in the process.

Table 4: Inner Texture of 2 Samuel 11:6-13

Verse	Repetitive texture	Opening–Middle–Closing	Progressive texture
6	David (2x), Joab (2x), Uriah (2x), sent (2x)/send	11:6 So David sent word to Joab	David, send, sent
7	David, Joab, Uriah		Came, asked, going
8	David, king (2x), Uriah	David said to Uriah, "Go down to your house"	Go down, went out

Verse	Repetitive texture	Opening–Middle–Closing	Progressive texture
9	Uriah, his (2x), king/lord		Did not go down
10	David (2x), Uriah (x2)		Not go down, not come, not go down
11	Uriah, David/lord, Joab, my (4x)		Shall I then go, I will not
12	David, Uriah (2x)		Remain here, send you back, Uriah remained
13	David/lord, him (2x), he (4x), his (3x)	... but he did not go down to his house.	Invited, drank, drunk, lie, not go down

On the surface, it seems as if Uriah was simply a good officer who would never violate military protocol for the sake of self-indulgence. However, it is clear that the author intentionally left gaps in the narrative to allow David's behavior to speak for itself. For example, David sent Joab to retrieve Uriah, but then David asked Uriah about Joab's well-being "and how the people were doing and how the war was going" (2 Sam 11:7). If David wanted to know how things were going, he could have asked his top official Joab (Andrews & Bergen, 2009). Thus, it seems evident that David already had his heart set on covering up his affair with Bathsheba by using Uriah's behavior as a husband to either mask David's paternity or to set some sort of snare Uriah. Although the narrative is full of gaps, the author used the drama of conversation and multiple perspectives to map out David's plan for Uriah (Sternberg, 1987). For example, instead of the author plainly stating David's desire to cover up the affair, the author used David's offerings of respite as a typology of the same temptation David initially faced in Section 2. However, unlike David who gave in to temptation to satisfy his own desires and ease his own *war wounds*, Uriah rejected pleasure for the sake of his commitment to Israel. Thus, it is through David's *back and forth* with Uriah that the reader realizes that David is dedicated to covering up the affair no matter what the cost.

The social and cultural texture of Section 3 offers great insight into David's frame of mind and Uriah's morality. As mentioned, Uriah the Hittite was one of David's *mighty men*. However, Uriah was a foreigner. In Section 2, David presented three gifts to Uriah, and each time Uriah refused to compromise his morals. For example, David commanded Uriah: "Go down to your house and wash your feet" (2 Sam 11:7). Some have suggested that the term *wash your feet* means enjoy a time of refreshment, while others have suggested that *feet* is a euphemism for genitalia, which underscores the sexual nature of David's order (Andrews & Bergen, 2009; Gordon, 1999). Gordon (1999) argued that *wash your feet* could also "refer to a ritual ablution releasing a soldier from the vow of sexual abstinence during a military campaign" (p. 254). The Hebrew Law explicitly equated sexual activity with ceremonial uncleanness (Lev 15:16). Furthermore, David's armies were always sexually inactive during active military duty as displayed in 1 Samuel 21:5: And David answered the priest, "Truly women have been kept from us as always when I go on an expedition. The vessels of the young men are holy even when it is an ordinary journey. How much more today will their vessels be holy?"

This not only further illustrates the depths of David's sin, it also highlights the contrast in morality between David of Israel and Uriah the Hittite. Herein lies a subtle intertextual layer. Even Uriah's name contains the short form of Israel's holiest name, Yahweh, which further adds to the irony of David's behavior (Gordon, 1999). Andrews and Bergen (2009) argued that Uriah knew that violating the sexual purity code of Israel's army could not only carry the death sentence, it could also result in God opposing the Israelite army on the battlefield (Josh 7:1-12). Instead of going home to *wash his feet*, Uriah slept in the open with the servants (2 Sam 11:9). When David inquired as to Uriah's rejection of the gift of home and Bathsheba, Uriah appealed to the highest morality: God (2 Sam 11:11). Baldwin (2008) argued that Uriah's mentioning of the Ark, Israel, and Judah not only paints a stark contrast between David and Uriah, it also highlights the Levitical underpinnings of Uriah's ethical framework.

This has implications for the sacred texture of Section 3. Instead of David realizing how far his values had shifted from the law of God, David ordered Uriah to remain in Jerusalem for another evening of food, drink, and pleasure (2 Sam 11:12-13). Scholars have agreed that this final order was designed to exploit Uriah's drunkenness with the hope that Uriah would indeed go home and *wash his feet and* have sexual intercourse with Bathsheba (Andrews & Bergen, 2009; Baldwin, 2008; Gordon, 1999). However, the chronology of the narrative suggests that David's plot was more than just a plot for Uriah to impregnate Bathsheba. Based on the information found in Section 1 and Section 2, Bathsheba would have been well on her way to at least 2 months pregnant by the time David's initial plot came to fruition. David sent a messenger to retrieve Uriah from Rabbah, which is approximately 40 miles away from Jerusalem if one were to travel using the shortest distance (Beitzel, 2009). Since the terrain between Rabbah and Jerusalem is hilly and rugged, and since there were few established roads directly linking the two cities, one could argue that it took several days for the messenger to reach Joab and Uriah and several more days for Uriah to return to Jerusalem (Beitzel, 2009). According to Gabriel (2003), "The most direct road from Jerusalem to Rabbah crossed the Jordan just north of the Dead Sea and proceeded east via Heshbon" (p. 262). Although this road late proved advantageous for Joab's rapid assault, at least 25 miles of the road was through open country, which made it the perfect place for an ambush (Gabriel, 2003). For example, Joab's massive army was immediately ambushed upon arrival in Rabbah (2 Sam 10:8-10; Gabriel, 2003). Thus, messengers traveling this route would have to take great caution since they would not have the full support of an advancing Army for security. An argument can be made that had Uriah gone home and *washed his feet*, David could have disavowed the order and had Uriah executed for violating the law of God and the protocols of David's army regarding sexual purity, since it may have been hard to convince Uriah and others that Bathsheba was not already pregnant. Thus, the climax of cultural and social tension takes place within Section 3 as demonstrated in David's hidden unethical and immoral exchange with Uriah.

In summary, Section 3 contains three critical insights for ethical and moral leadership. First, there is a clear connection between David's compromised moral foundation and his unethical decision making. David's willingness to manipulate and exploit his servants, Uriah's emotions, and Uriah's standing as a leader in the Israelite army all underscore the drift in David's moral compass. Second, although it appears as if David is calculating and intentional in Section 3, the evidence suggests that David is also functioning in an irrational state. This erratic behavior could stem from David's desperation, or it could be a further symptom of his underlying stress. Finally, the evidence shows that David's compromised morality caused him to disregard anyone else's moral compass.

CHAPTER 9

David Starts Killing - 2 Samuel 11:14-25

2 Samuel 11:14-25

There are multiple textual layers to consider in Section 4. In verses 14-25, the author illustrated just how far David was willing to go in order to cover up his affair with Bathsheba. Section 4 presents David as a cold, calculating, and mad king bent on self-preservation no matter the moral or tactical price. Furthermore, the author introduced another point of contrast in Section 4 by comparing the morals and ethics of Joab with the morals and ethics of King David. According to Robbins (1996a), the sensory–aesthetic texture deals with three body zones: (a) emotion-fused thought, (b) self-expressive speech, and (c) purposeful action. The sensory–aesthetic of Section 4 includes references to the time of day, the ferocity of fight at Rabbah, and the actions of the combatants during the siege. The author maintained an objective and *matter of fact* tone throughout the section in order to avoid biasing the reader (Sternberg, 1987). However, within the social and cultural texture of the periscope, one is able to fill in the gaps regarding the details of the siege of Rabbah.

After Uriah refused to fall into David's trap, the king wrote a letter to Joab with a "deadly plan" (Andrews & Bergen, 2009, p. 273) designed to once and for all resolve the Uriah problem. Joab was located on the front lines in Rabbah. The siege of Rabbah was a campaign against the Ammonites and part of David's larger campaign against the Arameans (Gabriel, 2003). According to 2 Samuel 10:1-8, the Aramean war was a tactical response to failed diplomacy, blatant insult, and an ever increasing threat to Israel's eastern borders. Gabriel (2003) suggested that David's previous victories during the Philistine campaign led the Aramean coalition to mobilize against Israel in order to gain access to the Transjordan and control of the King's Highway, which was a critical trade route in the ANE. In response to this mobilized coalition, David led the entire might of the Israelite army to attack the Aramean coalition. One year after the victories outlined in 2 Samuel 10:1-19, David sent Joab and all of Israel to directly attack the capital of Ammon: Rabbah. However, David stayed in Jerusalem.

Previous sections have already explored the ethical and moral significance of David's decision to stay in Jerusalem. However, Section 4 offers insight into the tactical and executive leadership issues associated with David's decision to stay in Jerusalem. Herein also lies the connection between Section 1 and the primary research question of this study: Why did David stay in Jerusalem? Since kings typically went to war in the spring time, and since the literal translation of *the time when kings go to war* is *litshubat hashana* or *the return of the year*, and since Israel had an established forward operating base 25 miles northwest of Ammon in Succoth, and since 1 year had passed since David's initial victory over the Aramean coalition (2 Sam 10:17-19), it is evident that David stayed in Jerusalem to avoid personally going into battle (2 Sam 11:1; Gabriel, 2003, p. 267). David could have marched out with Israel as was his custom and the evidence suggests that he may have been present during the initial Aramean campaign. David also could have led the siege of Rabbah from the relative safety of the forward operating base Succoth. Instead, David stayed in Jerusalem and sent Joab out with the entire army to attack the Ammonite capital.

According to the text, Joab had already successfully "ravaged the Ammonites" (2 Sam 11:1). With the capital under siege, all Joab and the Army had to do was wait out the soon-to-be starving residents of Rabbah while simultaneously keeping any outside help from reaching Rabbah (Andrews & Bergen, 2009). This type of classic besiegement was normal in ancient warfare (Andrews & Bergen, 2009). However, David's letter to Joab and Joab's response indicate a series of tactical shifts and errors that are directly related to David's cover-up. It is critical to note that Uriah delivered David's instructions in a sealed document to Joab. Thus, David had Uriah carry his own death sentence. This further demonstrates the damage done to David's moral and ethical foundation. David instructed Joab to "Set Uriah in the forefront of the hardest fighting, and then draw back from him, that he may be struck down, and die" (2 Sam 11:15). However, the next two verses show that Joab did not carry out David's order:

> And as Joab was besieging the city, he assigned Uriah to the place where he knew there were valiant men. And the men of the city came out and fought with Joab, and some of the servants of David among the people fell. Uriah the Hittite also died. (2 Sam 11:16-17).

Scholars have been at odds as to why David's order was not carried out by Joab in exact fashion. Gabriel (2003) argued that Israel had abandoned siege tactics and was committed to taking Rabbah by way of *old school* brute force. Thus, Joab would not need to place Uriah were the fighting was the fiercest because such a place did not exist. Campbell (2005) suggested that upon receiving David's order, Joab put the pieces together and knew that David had cause to execute Uriah, yet for some reason David needed to conceal the execution. Thus, if Joab had carried out the order exactly as instructed, it would have been difficult for Joab and David to cover up the blatant murder of a respected Israelite officer (Campbell, 2005). Moreover, the intense loyalty of David's mighty men may have fueled a mass mutiny had the soldiers known about the murder plot. According to Sternberg (1987), Joab covered the holes in David's murder plot by provoking "a sharp battle in which many are killed" (p. 214) to bury the murder of Uriah in a narrative of death amongst comrades. Gordon (1999) suggested that as David's most loyal accomplice, Joab understood the "spirit of the royal letter" (p. 255) and adjusted the plan in a way that would accomplish David's mission while also eliminating and witnesses to David's treacherousness. All of these theories suggest that David's compromised ethical framework had a direct impact on the ethical decision making of his subordinates, namely Joab. Both Uriah and Joab were more than just pawns in King David's vast army. As mentioned previously, both played critical roles in the executive leadership of Israel's armies. However, Uriah proved to be an exception to the ethical compromise demonstrated by David and Joab. The evidence suggests that by refusing to *wash his feet*, Uriah demonstrated a higher ethic than David. The rest of Section 4 provides evidence that suggests Joab may not have been as interested in covering David's tracks as he was in teaching the king a lesson through unethical methods.

The sending of a courier back and forth between the battlefield and the king was common in the ANE (Andrews & Bergen, 2009). Rather than sending a letter to the king, Joab chose to send messenger with a detailed account of the battle. Sternberg (1987) suggested that the use of a messenger was a matter of pragmatism: Joab did not have time to draft and seal a manuscript. However, it is important to note that Joab did not want to risk anything being lost in translation. Thus, Joab *coached* the messenger with full expectation that David would be angry to hear about the loss of life during the battle:

> And he instructed the messenger, "When you have finished telling all the news about the fighting to the king, then, if the king's anger rises, and if he says to you, 'Why did you go so near the city to fight? Did you not know that they would shoot from the wall? Who killed Abimelech the son of Jerubbesheth? Did not a woman cast an upper millstone on him from the wall, so that he died at Thebez? Why did you go so near the wall?' then you shall say, 'Your servant Uriah the Hittite is dead also.'" (2 Sam 11:19-21)

Some have suggested that Joab used poor tactics to mask the murder of Uriah (Andrews & Bergen, 2009; Sternberg, 1987). Campbell (2005) suggested that Joab purposefully moved the troops into harm's way to mask David's ruthlessness. Both arguments are supported by the evidence. However, Joab's reference to Judges 9:50-57, which represents the only pure intertextual layer in the entire passage, offers insight into his ethical framework. Judges 9:50-57 is part of the DH and tells the story of the death of Abimelech, the sixth Judge of Israel and the only judge to achieve power through unethical and immoral means (Judg 9:1-6). According to Judges 9:50-57,

> Then Abimelech went to Thebez and encamped against Thebez and captured it. But there was a strong tower within the city, and all the men and women and all the leaders of the city fled to it and shut themselves in, and they went up

to the roof of the tower. And Abimelech came to the tower and fought against it and drew near to the door of the tower to burn it with fire. And a certain woman threw an upper millstone on Abimelech's head and crushed his skull. Then he called quickly to the young man his armor-bearer and said to him, "Draw your sword and kill me, lest they say of me, 'A woman killed him.'" And his young man thrust him through, and he died. And when the men of Israel saw that Abimelech was dead, everyone departed to his home. Thus God returned the evil of Abimelech, which he committed against his father in killing his seventy brothers. And God also made all the evil of the men of Shechem return on their heads, and upon them came the curse of Jotham the son of Jerubbaal.

According to Baldwin (2008), Joab "knew better than to go so close to the wall" ("David's Adultery," para. 10). However, David created an ethical conflict for Joab by issuing a written order to passively execute Uriah. Therefore, instead of letting the narrative shift from David's immorality toward Joab's tactical incompetence, Joab decided to insert a story from Israel's past into the mind of the messenger and into the mind of David to subtly remind the king that he was aware of the king's ethical failings (Baldwin, 2008). In the same way that Abimelech was destroyed by treachery and a woman, David was also at risk of being destroyed by treachery and a woman. The evidence suggests that Joab was aware of David's affair and used the unethical tactic of sacrificing the lives of Israel's soldiers in order to fulfill David's execution order while also teaching David a lesson.

According to the Scriptures, the messenger delivered Joab's report to David in its entirety (2 Sam 11:22-24). In some ways, the messengers represent a form of detachment between the chief moral and ethical agents of the narrative and the consequences of unethical and immoral behavior. David used the written word to carry out a personal attack against Uriah, and Joab used the spoken word to respond to the king's attack. However, by sending a messenger, neither party has to come face to face with the ethical dilemma. There is not enough evidence to suggests that the messengers are ethical or moral agents in the passage.

The message in verses 22-25 included news that there was a large loss of life amongst the king's servants. The Greek translation of the Old Testament, which is known as the Septuagint, contains an extended version of verse 22 that includes David referring to Judges 9:50-57 just as Joab predicted (Gordon, 1999). David was unaware of Joab's alterations to the execution order regarding Uriah. Thus, it is logical to assume that David would have been angry upon hearing about the loss of his servants and Joab's tactical blunder (Gabriel, 2003; Sternberg, 1987). However, upon hearing the full story, David did not respond in anger and blame Joab. Instead, David viewed the tactical failure as an acceptable loss of life because Joab's tactical error had accomplished David's ultimate plan of eliminating Uriah. David's reply serves as the *rock bottom* in his moral and ethical descent: David said to the messenger, "Thus shall you say to Joab, 'Do not let this matter displease you, for the sword devours now one and now another. Strengthen your attack against the city and overthrow it.' And encourage him" (2 Sam 11:25).

Baldwin (2008) suggested this is the point at which David begins the process of "placating his own conscience" ("David's Adultery," para. 12) by taking the posture of a caring and humble superior officer. According to Campbell (2005), "With the news of Uriah's death, anger is replaced with ruthlessness" ("Chapter 6 Discussion," para. 14) as the David, who inspired deep loyalty, becomes "ruthlessly disloyal" ("Chapter 6 Discussion," para. 14). Andrews and Bergen (2009) argued that David responded to the news of the failed battle philosophically because he knew that his plan to cover his own immorality had actually succeeded. Instead of mourning the loss of so many lives, mourning the loss of one of his chief officials, and repenting of his treacherous behavior, David "played the role of a pastoral counselor" (Andrews & Bergen, 2009, p. 274) and encouraged Joab to regroup and assault with the full support of the king and all of Israel. The inner texture of Section 4 reveals how the author used multiple characters to underscore the moral decline of King David.

In summary, Section 4 contains several insights for ethical and moral leadership. First, ethical behavior trickles down through an organization. David's coldness in his order to have Uriah killed is reflected in Joab's coldness toward the servants of David, many of whom were sacrificed in order to kill Uriah. Second, unethical behavior produces detachment and rationalization. Both David and Uriah used messengers and the actions of others to create distance between their own unethical behavior and the consequences of those actions. Finally, David's response to the news regarding Uriah's death demonstrates the length that an immoral and unethical leader is willing to go in order to *move on* from their mistakes.

Table 5: Inner Texture of 2 Samuel 11:14-25

Verse	Repetitive texture	Opening–Middle–Closing	Progressive texture
14	David, Joab, Uriah, wrote, sent	11:6 In the morning David wrote a letter	David, wrote, sent
15	He (David), Uriah		Wrote, set, draw back, die
16	Joab, he, Uriah		Besiege, assign
17	Men, servants, Joab, David, Uriah		Came, fought, fell
18	Joab, David	11:18 Then Joab sent and told David all the news	Sent, told
19	He, messenger, king		Finished telling
20	King, he		Anger rises, he says
21	Abimelech, woman, he, him, you (2x), Uriah		Who killed, did not, why did
22	Messenger, David, Joab, him		Went, told all
23	Messenger, David, men, us (2x), we,		Came out, drove back
24	Archers, servants (3x), king's, Uriah		Shot at, dead, dead also
25	David, messenger, you (2x), Joab, your, him	11:25 Do not let this matter displease you	Say to, strengthen attack, encourage him

CHAPTER 10

David Covers It Up - 2 Samuel 11:26-27

2 Samuel 11:26-27

The final section of the passage is just as direct as the first section. Although Section 5 only consists of two verses, the textual layers of both verses offer insight into David's ethical and moral decision making. The inner texture of Section 5 contains several of the same patterns and themes found in the previous sections.

Table 6: Inner Texture of 2 Samuel 11:26-27

Verse	Repetitive texture	Opening–Middle–Closing	Progressive texture
26	Wife, she, her (2x), Uriah (2x), husband	11:26 When the wife of Uriah heard	Heard, lamented
27	David (2x), his, him, her, she, wife	But the thing that David had done displeased the Lord.	Sent, brought, became, displeased

In verse 26, the author reintroduces Bathsheba as a key character in the narrative. Unlike David, Uriah, and Joab, Bathsheba only has one line of dialogue in the entire passage (2 Sam 11:5). Furthermore, the voice of Bathsheba is not heard again until near the end of David's life (1 Kings 1:31). Yet, verse 26 contains key information that informs the reader as to

Bathsheba's disposition during David's unethical and immoral behavior regarding Uriah: "When the wife of Uriah heard that Uriah her husband was dead, she lamented over her husband" (2 Sam 11:26). The evidence suggests that, once again, a messenger played a critical role in the unfolding of the narrative. Although the text is unclear as to *who* Bathsheba heard from, the text clearly states Bathsheba's response to the news.

Ceremonial mourning was a common and meticulous process in the ANE, which included at least 7 days of fasting, lamentation, and modified appearance (Gordon, 1999). However, the text does not suggest that Bathsheba's mourning was out of a deep devotion to Uriah before or after her affair with David (Gordon, 1999). According to Baldwin (2008), the phrase *wife of Uriah* is used in verse 26 as a way of reminding the reader of the depth of David's sin and to pay respect to the man who acted with honor as opposed to the dishonorable David and Joab. Respect and honor are both critical elements of the final two verses of this passage. Bathsheba mourned Uriah because that was the honorable and expected practice of the day. This further confirms Bathsheba's posture as one who typically behaved according to the religious and moral customs of the day.

Verse 27 provides the reader with David's response to the situation: "And when the mourning was over, David sent and brought her to his house, and she became his wife and bore him a son" (1 Sam 11:27a). Andrews and Bergen (2009) suggested that David "was playing the role of a *go'el*—a kinsman redeemer (Deut 25:5-6; Rth 3:1-4:6)—by taking on the obligation" (p. 274) of marrying, caring for, and impregnating Bathsheba. According to tradition, one of the duties of the *go'el* was to provide the widow with a child (Andrews & Bergen, 2009). With Uriah dead, David took advantage of both tradition and the situation he had created to officially make Bathsheba his wife. Ironically, this was not the first time David had taken on the role of a kinsman redeemer. In 1 Samuel 25:39-42, the author of the DH shared another story involving David, ethics, and another man's wife:

> When David heard that Nabal was dead, he said, "Blessed be
> the Lord who has avenged the insult I received at the hand
> of Nabal, and has kept back his servant from wrongdoing.
> The Lord has returned the evil of Nabal on his own head."
> Then David sent and spoke to Abigail, to take her as his wife.

When the servants of David came to Abigail at Carmel, they said to her, "David has sent us to you to take you to him as his wife." And she rose and bowed with her face to the ground and said, "Behold, your handmaid is a servant to wash the feet of the servants of my lord." And Abigail hurried and rose and mounted a donkey, and her five young women attended her. She followed the messengers of David and became his wife.

Although it is beyond the scope of this research to thoroughly analyze 1 Samuel 25:25-39-42, it is important to note the parallel themes regarding *messengers, sending, wrongdoing,* and ethics that exist in both passages. In David's encounter with Abigail, it is David who suffered wrongdoing by the hand of Nabal (1 Sam 25:1-11), whereas in David's encounter with Bathsheba, it is Uriah who suffers wrongdoing at the hand of David. Both situations resulted in David acquiring a wife upon the death of her husband. Berger (2009) argued that the author of the Book of Ruth had prior knowledge of the DH and set forth to redeem the unethical behavior of David by presenting David's great-grandfather Boaz as a moral kinsman redeemer.

Regardless of David's motives in ultimately marrying Bathsheba, the author presented the final indictment of David's behavior: "But the thing that David had done displeased the Lord" (2 Sam 11:27b). Not until the very end of the passage did the author finally provide the reader with a "moral evaluation" (Sternberg, 1987, p. 218) of David's behavior. Yet, the author was not clear in 2 Samuel 11 as to which *thing* displeased the Lord. Since taking the role of a kinsman redeemer was a common and approved practice amongst the Hebrew people, and since widowed women were not forbidden from remarriage, it is safe to assume that the *thing* that displeased the Lord was David's adulterous murder of Uriah and not his marriage to Bathsheba. However, in 2 Samuel 12:9-12 the Prophet Nathan specified the *things* that displeased the Lord along with the consequences for David's actions:

Why have you despised the word of the Lord, to do what is evil in his sight? You have struck down Uriah the Hittite with the sword and have taken his wife to be your wife and have killed him with the sword of the Ammonites. Now therefore the sword shall never depart from your house, because you have despised me and have taken the wife of Uriah the Hittite to be your wife. Thus says the Lord, "Behold, I will raise up evil against you out of your own house. And I will take your wives before your eyes and give them to your neighbor, and he shall lie with your wives in the sight of this sun. For you did it secretly, but I will do this thing before all Israel and before the sun."

Thus, David displeased the Lord by (a) despising the word of the Lord, (b) conspiring to do evil, (c) murdering Uriah, (d) using the enemy to accomplish murder, and (e) taking Uriah's wife (2 Sam 12:9). The immediate and long-term consequences of God's displeasure with David are detailed in 2 Samuel 12-19 and summarized in Table 7.

Table 7: Consequences of David's Unethical Behavior

Chapter	Consequence	David's response
2 Sam 12:1-14	David exposed and rebuked by Nathan the Prophet	Repentance
2 Sam 12:16-17	David and Bathsheba's unnamed child becomes sick	Prayer and Fasting
2 Sam 12:18-25	David and Bathsheba's unnamed child dies	Acceptance, comfort of Bathsheba, Solomon born
2 Sam 13:1-22	David's daughter Tamar raped by her brother Amnon	Anger and inaction
2 Sam 13:23-33	David's son Absalom murders his brother Amnon	Bitter mourning for Amnon, longing for Absalom
2 Sam 15:1-37	Absalom conspires to overthrow David	Flee from Jerusalem

Chapter	Consequence	David's response
2 Sam 16:15-23	Absalom enters Jerusalem and publicly sleeps with David's concubines	Inaction
2 Sam 18:1-33	Absalom killed in battle	Bitter mourning for Absalom
2 Sam 19:1-43	Joab rebukes David, potential for mutiny	Encourage the people, pardon enemies

In summary, Section 5 contains multiple observations relating to ethical and moral leadership. First, unethical behavior and decision has an immediate impact on the various parties involved in the behavior. David's decision to murder Uriah instantly made Bathsheba a widow. Second, unethical behavior has the potential for long-term negative consequences. David's behavior forever altered the trajectory of his dynasty and produced a family culture of incest, sexual immorality, treachery, murder, and division. Finally, unethical behavior displeases the Lord. Although this final theological point may seem irrelevant to the unreligious, it should serve as a foundational truth for Christian leaders.

Summary

The entire text of 2 Samuel 11:1-27 has been explored using sociorhetorical analysis for the purpose of examining what, if any, connections exist between the passage and ethical and moral decision making and behavior. Emphasis was given to the role of leadership fatigue and trauma in ethical decision making. The analysis was conducted from a theological and philosophical framework in which the Hebrew and Christian Scriptures are considered the primary source of all that is ethical and moral. The in-depth analysis produced several recurring themes that have implications for modern leadership contexts. The most prominent themes found in the analysis were (a) stress, (b) cover-ups, (c) intermediaries, and (d) honor and dishonor.

The first and central theme in the passage is the often overlooked presence of stress. The context of the passage centers on environmental, psychosocial, and emotional stress. In the opening verses, the author plainly stated that King David is in the middle of a military campaign, which one could argue only added to the stress of leading the day-to-day governmental activities of Israel. Since David chose to remain in Jerusalem, and since David remained in a constant war footing, and since the trauma of warfare leads to stress, it is safe to assume that David may have remained in Jerusalem in order to deal with the stress of war. Moreover, David's repeated attempts to hide his ethical failures are precipitated by the stress of his being *found out*. Thus, the theme of stress played an important role in David's ethical and moral decision making.

Another theme that is prevalent in the passage is the concept of the *cover-up*. Instead of immediately confessing his sins regarding Bathsheba, King David attempted to cover up the affair by having Uriah break his vow of abstinence. David covered up this initial plot by offering Uriah gifts, respite, and the allusion of a caring leader. When the initial plot failed, David attempted to cover up Bathsheba's pregnancy by having Uriah murdered on the battlefield. Having identified the flaws in David's plan, Joab covered for the king by manipulating the battle in such a manner as to mask Uriah death with the death of a multitude of Israelite warriors. Finally, David comforted and married Bathsheba as a final way of covering up the entire series of unethical and immoral behaviors.

There are 21 references to either a *messenger* or one being *sent* in the 27 verses of 1 Samuel 11. Thus, the theme of the *intermediary* is extensive throughout the passage. It is important to note that the use of messengers was a common practice in the ANE (Sternberg, 1987). However, it is also important to note how the use of *messengers* always places an intermediary between the ethical agents of the passage and the victims of the unethical and immoral behavior. David used a messenger to send for Bathsheba and to send for Uriah, and he used Uriah to carry out his own death sentence. Joab used messengers to communicate to the king, and he used the lives of several Israelite warriors to create distance between the king and Uriah's murder. Furthermore, Bathsheba used intermediaries to express her pregnancy and sorrow.

Finally, the entire passage deals with the themes of honor and dishonor. It is clear that David's repeated attempts at covering up his unethical behavior were attempts to preserve his own honor and ultimately the honor of Israel as a nation. However, since his behavior was contrary to the moral laws of God, it is also clear that David did not attempt to honor the God of Israel during this season of his life. The author consistently compared and contrasted the dishonorable behavior of David with the honorable behavior of Uriah. Almost ironically, Joab honored King David by showing dishonor to Uriah the Hittite and a multitude of Israelite warriors. Furthermore, David appeared to honor the Hebrew tradition by becoming a *go'el* for Bathsheba, even though his dishonorable behavior created Bathsheba's problems.

CHAPTER 11

Lessons From An Old King

The findings in the text of 2 Samuel 11:1-27 reveal five principles for ethical and moral leadership: (a) leadership is not only hard, it is traumatic; (b) accountability is an ethical force multiplier; (c) failure is fatal, but not final; (d) ethical and moral decision making is a 360-degree process; and (e) everything rises and falls on theology. First, the opening verses of the passage place David's leadership within the context of war and stress. Furthermore, these verses reveal a break in David's normal behavioral patterns. David was historically an upright and ethical leader. He had developed a reputation of righteousness. However, years of prolonged warfare coupled with the establishment and maintenance of the unified Israelite nation had obviously taken a toll on David's soul and psyche. Therefore, it is apparent that the presence of stress when compounded with untreated emotional and psychological trauma has a negative impact on a leader's ability to make ethical and moral decisions. David's behavior in the passage is so out of character that there are no other reasonable explanations for why he behaved in such a treacherous manner. This is not to say that every unethical decision will result in adultery or murder. However, it is clear that one seemingly innocuous decision can have serious consequences if left unchecked by a strong ethical and moral compass. Thus, for David, leadership was not only hard it was also traumatic.

The passage also reveals that David operated outside of the guardrails of accountability. As commander in chief and chief executive of Israel, David had no peers or authority to submit to beyond the Law of Moses and the customs of Israel. The *weight* of leadership, especially in isolation took a toll on David's spirituality and ultimately his moral compass. The *voice of reason* demonstrated in 2 Samuel 12 was silent in 2 Samuel 11. However, as soon as David was confronted by the Prophet Nathan in 2 Samuel 12, David repented of his wrongdoing. According to the U.S. Joint Chiefs of Staff (2014), a force multiplier is "a capability that, when added to and employed by a combat force, significantly increases the combat potential of that force and thus enhances the probability of successful mission accomplishment" (p. GL-7). However, the term force multiplier is frequently used across multiple disciplines to refer to anything that may increase the effectiveness of something else (T. C. Allen, 2014). Since David had a previous reputation as being one who honored the laws of God; and since David seemed receptive to correction and accountability; and since David had access to all of the prophets, scribes, and leaders in Israel, it is safe to assume that accountability would have increased David's ability to function in an ethical and moral manner. Therefore, accountability is a force multiplier. Thus, it is clear that had David given room for accountability earlier on, his affair with Bathsheba and the subsequent cover-up may have been avoided.

David's unethical decision making resulted in the literal death of Uriah, David and Bathsheba's unnamed child, and a large number of Israelite warriors. His actions also resulted in the figurative death of the unified Israelite kingdom. However, even though David's failures produced fatalities, they also set the stage for redemption and new birth (2 Sam 12:24-25; Psalm 89:3-4, 132:11-12; Luk 1:32-33). Thus, it is clear that although one may never escape the consequences of unethical and immoral decision making, there is always room for something good to *rise from the ashes* of leadership failure. In this way, ethical failure will result in the death of something, be it one's reputation or, in extreme cases, the literal death of another person. Nevertheless, there is also room for one to grow morally and ethically in response to ethical and moral failure.

Furthermore, ethical leadership does not exist on an island of isolation. Although David's decision to stay in Jerusalem, his decision to send for Bathsheba, his decision to involve Joab, and his decision to kill Uriah were all rooted in self-centeredness and self-preservation, his ethics had a direct impact on multiple people both inside and outside of his organization. The consequences of unethical and immoral leadership are both immediate and long-lasting. There is no guarantee that a change of attitude and a posture of repentance will undue the results of unethical leadership or stop future consequences. So, it is clear that the concepts of leadership fatigue, ethical leadership, and moral leadership operate in a 360-degree manner as opposed to a linear top-down manner.

Finally, ethical and moral leadership are fundamentally theological constructs. David had a pattern of fulfilling his religious duties and trusting in God for help, especially deliverance from his enemies (Psalm 24, 34, 52, 54, 56, 59, 60, 96, 105-106). However, it is evident that leadership fatigue played a role in disconnecting David from his theologically oriented moral compass. David had several opportunities to repent and change course, and every time he chose to head farther into unethical and immoral behavior. Therefore, it is clear that leadership fatigue impacts one's soul before it impacts one's decision making. When it comes to understanding morality and ethics and subsequently behaving in an ethical manner, everything rises and falls on theology.

This book sought to answer five questions:

1. What moral and ethical decisions did David make in 2 Samuel 11:1-27?
2. Why did David make these decisions?
3. What prior trauma or stress influenced David's decisions?
4. Does this passage offer insight into modern ethical and moral leadership theories?
5. Are there implications for Christian leadership found within this passage?

Furthermore, this book sought to demonstrate that sociorhetorical analysis is an effective methodology for organizational leadership research. The author of the passage wrote to a Hebrew audience for the purpose of re-teaching the history of Israel to a postexilic generation. In the process, the author did not shy away from a *dark* chapter in the life of Israel's greatest king. However, the author did not explicitly assign ethical or moral value to David's decision making and behavior until the final verse of the passage. Therefore, in order to examine the role of leadership fatigue and trauma in David's ethical and moral decision making, it was necessary to explore the entire passage from multiple textual layers.

Question 1

Question 1 explored what, if any, moral and ethical decisions were made by David in 2 Samuel 11:1-27. According to the results of the study, David made several ethical and moral decisions in the passage. Since moral knowledge influences ethical behavior, it is evident that the first moral decisions that David made were to forsake his deep understanding of the Law of Moses and his theologically inspired charge as king of Israel (Rae, 2009). Upon the compromise of David's moral foundation, his moral and ethical decision-making processes began to reflect the converse of the Law of Moses. David decided to stay in Jerusalem, which led to his lusting after Bathsheba, which led to his committing adultery with Bathsheba, which led to his deceit and attempted entrapment toward Uriah the Hittite, which led to his direct role in the murder of Uriah. Furthermore, David influenced the sinful behavior Joab, who sacrificed the lives of innocent Israelite warriors in an attempt to aid the king's cover-up. However, not all of David's ethical and moral decisions were negative. In the end, David chose to comfort and marry Bathsheba, which ultimately led to the redemptive narrative of this chapter in David's life. Thus, Research Question 1 was correct in its assumption that David made several ethical and moral decisions as seen in the passage. Moreover, this further substantiates the Hebrew Scriptures as being a valuable source for leadership research. This is also valuable since the entire study builds on the foundation of ethical and moral leadership.

Question 2

The study successfully answered Question 2, which sought to answer the *why* questions behind David's moral and ethical decisions as seen in the passage. However, the results of the study reveal that there is little explicit evidence in the passage to answer questions relating to *why* David chose to stay in Jerusalem, *why* he chose to commit adultery with Bathsheba, or *why* he married Bathsheba in the end. According to Patton (2002), hermeneutics involves the reconstructing of reality on the basis of interpretation, which "occurs within a tradition" (p. 115) and involves the perspectives of the interpreter and the participation of the original source of data. Since King David is obviously unavailable for questioning, and since 2 Samuel 11 is intentionally vague when it comes to motive, it is difficult to make definitive claims as to *why* David chose to stay in Jerusalem based on a one-dimensional reading of the text (Sternberg, 1987). However, based on the in-depth and multidimensional sociorhetorical analysis of 2 Samuel 11, it is plausible that David chose to stay in Jerusalem because of burnout, trauma, or fatigue associated with executive leadership and a constant state of combat.

Furthermore, it is also clear that the rest of David's unethical and immoral decisions were probably motivated by self-preservation. David either sought to maintain his moral and executive authority in Israel by way of cover-up or he sought to spare Israel the embarrassment of scandal. Either way, the evidence suggests that David did not act with the interest of others in mind during his affair with Bathsheba and his involvement in Uriah's murder. According to the literature, dehumanization, blame shifting, diffusion of responsibility, and the abuse of power and privilege are all related to the impact of stress on ethical leadership (V. L. Allen, 2006; Bandura, 1999; Johnson, 2013). Thus, it is also clear that stress played a role in why David made a series of unethical and immoral decisions.

Question 3

Question 3 sought to explore what, if any, role stress had on David's moral and ethical decision making and behavior. According to the literature, religious leaders are highly susceptible to burnout (Hendron et al., 2012). Furthermore, the side effects of prolonged exposure to combat are restlessness, antisocial behavior, lapses in judgement, and a rationalization of inappropriate or inhumane behavior (Grossman, 2009; Regel & Joseph, 2010). The social and cultural analysis of the text revealed that David was more than likely a leader in the middle of burnout. This burnout could be the result of prolonged exposure to the trauma of combat, the pressure of establishing and maintaining the Hebrew capital of Israel, leading multiple military campaigns against a variety of hostile nations, overseeing the day-to-day governmental affairs of Israel, serving as the highest authority in Israel next to Jehovah, or a combination of the aforementioned. Based on the sociorhetorical evidence within the passage and the current literature on posttraumatic stress (PTS), burnout, and trauma, it is safe to assume that David may have suffered from posttraumatic stress disorder (PTSD).

Since David's decisions and behavior in 2 Samuel 11 represent an extreme departure from his normal character, it is clear that the presence of unchecked stress precipitated David's unethical and immoral decision making. Thus, Research Question 3 was answered in that a strong argument now exists for the evidence of leadership fatigue in David's life.

Question 4

Question 4 explored what, if any, connections exists between 2 Samuel 11 and modern ethical and moral leadership theories. David's behavior in the passage demonstrates a departure from the altruism and service associated with servant leadership and transformational leadership in that David did not consider the welfare of his followers above his own well-being (Northouse, 2015; Patterson, 2003). Furthermore, the self-seeking nature of David's behaviors in the passage confirm that David acted according to the principles of ethical egoism (Northouse, 2015). Finally, David's unethical behaviors influenced more unethical behavior in his followers, namely, Joab. Thus, this passage confirms the connection between perceived credibility, leadership, influence, and follower ethics (Brown, Treviño, et al., 2005; Yukl, 2013). The passage also demonstrates how unchecked stress and a lack of accountability may increase the probability of unethical and immoral decision making and behavior.

Question 5

Question 5 examined the implications of the study on Christian leadership. According to the literature, there is a link between morally intense situations, compassion fatigue, stress, and behavior (Diaconescu, 2015; Zheng et al., 2015). Furthermore, religious leaders are highly susceptible to compassion fatigue, secondary trauma, stress, and workplace burnout (Diaconescu, 2015; Grosch & Olsen, 2000; Hendron et al., 2012, 2014). The results of this study reveal four broad themes, which translate into five principles for ethical and moral leadership: (a) leadership is not only hard, it is traumatic; (b) accountability is an ethical force multiplier; (c) failure is fatal but not final; (d) ethical and moral decision making is a 360-degree process; and (e) everything rises and falls on theology. These principles have several implications for Christian leadership. Since Christian leaders are often exposed to trauma, stress, and morally intense situations; and since Christian leaders such as senior pastors often fulfill multiple vocational responsibilities; and since clergy are in a unique position to influence the ethics of others, it is paramount for ecclesial scholars to understand the effects of leadership fatigue on ethical and moral decision making. Furthermore, in view of the results of this study, it is important for Christian leaders to develop and employ practical safeguards against the effects of leadership fatigue. The principles developed from this study provide scholars and practitioners with a way forward in regards to ethical and moral decision making. The application of these principles may result in a reduction of ethical and moral failure amongst Christian leaders.

CHAPTER 12

Principles For New (and old) Leaders

Principle 1: Leadership is Hard and Traumatic

According to Maxwell (2007), personnel determine the potential of an organization, personal relationships determine the morale of an organization, systems and structures determine the size of an organization, and vision determines the direction of an organization. Furthermore, Maxwell argued, "Leadership determines the success of the organization... [because] everything rises and falls on leadership" ("Conclusion," para. 1). Moreover, leaders are expected to remain consistent in their abilities, even in environments of uncertainty (Tichy & McGill, 2003). Thus, by definition, leadership is *hard* because it requires that an individual possess a combination of traits and abilities that aid in the influence of follower behaviors and organizational outcomes. As mentioned, King David carried multiple *weights* relating to his role as the top leader in Israel. The results of this study reveal that along with the normal burdens associated with leadership, David also carried the unseen *weight* of trauma. Although the literature has given ample evidence to support the notion of leadership as being *hard*, the results of this study show a correlation between trauma and leadership. David was clearly impacted by his exposure to combat trauma, and the scope of his duties as king implies that he was also impacted by the intense pressure of executive leadership.

Furthermore, the results of this study and the existing literature relating to ethical and moral leadership suggest that leadership in and of itself is potentially traumatic. This means that the weight of leadership, when left unchecked, will produce negative consequences in a leader. For David, this meant participating in the dehumanizing, antisocial, and self-destructive behavior often associated with stress, PTS, and workplace burnout (DiGangi et al., 2013; Hendron et al., 2012, 2014; Regel & Joseph, 2010; Zheng et al., 2015). Figure 3 illustrates how the force and weight of the aforementioned variables influence a leader's ethical and moral decision-making process.

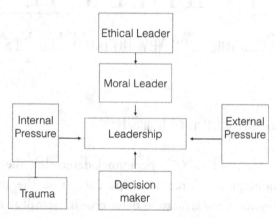

Figure 3: Principle 1—Leadership is hard and traumatic.

According to the literature, leaders are at the center of multiple variables, all of which have an impact on an organization's effectiveness (Kouzes & Posner, 2006; Yukl, 2013). Furthermore, leaders have a direct impact on the ethical and moral behavior of their followers (Schaubroek et al., 2002). Thus, leaders are called upon to serve as the chief ethical and moral leaders of their organizations while simultaneously carrying the burden of decision making. However, leaders also face the day-to-day external pressures of environmental uncertainty and the internal pressures associated with workplace stress and fatigue (DiGangi et al., 2013; Hendron et al., 2012, 2014; Tichy & McGill, 2003; Zheng et al., 2015). Moreover, the presence of preexisting mental health issues such as depression or burnout in a leader's life increase the negative effects associated with PTSD (Skogstad et al., 2013). Therefore, leadership is *hard* and *traumatic* because the combination of various weights and pressures are too much for one person to handle alone. This study revealed that King David's unethical behavior and immoral decision making were the result of leadership fatigue, which stemmed from the trauma of combat and the trauma of leadership.

Principle 2: Accountability is an Ethical Force Multiplier

There is a connection between accountability and ethical and moral decision making. By choosing to stay in Jerusalem instead of leading his forces into battle per his normal custom, David chose to isolate himself from those "who would normally serve as a firewall of accountability" (Plastow, 2016, p. 200), protecting him from inappropriate behavior. Isolation is one of the key symptoms of high levels of stress or untreated trauma. Leadership is a choice, and in 2 Samuel 11 it is evident that David compounded his unethical and immoral behavior by choosing isolation (Thistle & Molinaro, 2016). Ethical and moral excellence thrive in collaborative communities wherein leaders remain accountable to the constructs of ethical leadership and to the organizational communities in which they serve (Fluker, 2009). Since David responded to the rebuke of the Prophet Nathan, it is safe to assume that someone like Nathan could have served as a firewall for David had he or she been given the chance. Instead of choosing the collaborative community of accountability, David sought collaborators to help him mask his unethical behavior. The evidence suggests that had David sought out accountability through community, he may not have given into temptation and committed multiple offenses (Plastow, 2016). As illustrated in Figure 4, accountability multiplies the potential for ethical and moral behavior.

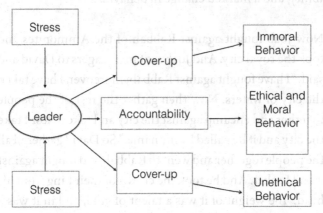

Figure 4: Principle 2—Accountability is a force multiplier.

Principle 3: Failure is Fatal but not Final

Ethical and moral failure in leadership has serious repercussions for both the leader and the organization. This type of failure not only produces reputation-damaging scandal, it also creates a series of new problems that must be overcome if an organization and its fallen leader are going to *bounce back*. Failure is fatal in that when a leader experiences a significant lapse in ethics and morality, something dies. The casualties of ethical failure range from the loss of reputation to the loss of valuable resources (Ludwig & Longenecker, 1993). In the case of David's failures, literal deaths resulted from his decision making and behavior. Indeed, David's leadership fatigue produced more stress and trauma in the lives of others. However, within the Judeo–Christian worldview, there is always room for redemption and rebirth. Furthermore, the author of the Deuteronomist History (DH) set out to present David as being a better king than Saul and Solomon, both of whom allowed poor ethics to ultimately define their leadership (Campbell & O'Brien, 2000; Peterson, 2014). Thus, although 2 Samuel 11 ends on a dark note, the rest of David's story shows that his ethical failure ultimately led to a rekindling and strengthening of his "commitment to God" (Plastow, 2016, p. 205) and a return to the values and ethics that defined much of his younger life. David's renewed ethic was the result of his repentance, submission to accountability, and a marked change in behavior:

> Now Joab fought against Rabbah of the Ammonites and took the royal city. And Joab sent messengers to David and said, "I have fought against Rabbah; moreover, I have taken the city of waters. Now then gather the rest of the people together and encamp against the city and take it, lest I take the city and it be called by my name." So David gathered all the people together and went to Rabbah and fought against it and took it. And he took the crown of their king from his head. The weight of it was a talent of gold, and in it was a precious stone, and it was placed on David's head. And he brought out the spoil of the city, a very great amount. And he brought out the people who were in it and set them to labor with saws and iron picks and iron axes and made them

toil at the brick kilns. And thus he did to all the cities of the
Ammonites. Then David and all the people returned to
Jerusalem. (2 Sam 12:26-31)

Therefore, even though there is a cost associated with ethical and moral
failure, there is also room for new opportunities, new growth, and a return to
an ethical *true north*. Figure 5 illustrates the two paths of ethical and moral
decision making.

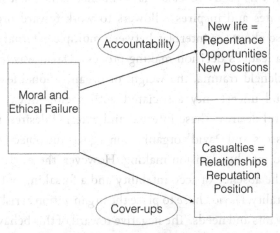

Figure 5: Principle 3—Failure is fatal but not final.

It is important to note that this principle is not drawn exclusively from 2
Samuel 11:1-27. The passage ends with David still in the activity of sinfulness.
However, since the study incorporated multiple passages from the DH as a
whole, and since Chapter 3 argued for the use of outside texts when necessary,
and since the literature has suggested that 2 Samuel 11 is part of a larger
apologetic for David as being God's king, and since David's affair with
Bathsheba set the stage for Israel's first royal dynasty, it is critical for this study
to highlight both the cost of David's failures and the redemption found within
the Davidic narrative (Berger, 2009; Rosenberg, 1989). This is especially
important since ethical and moral failure is far too often treated as either an
inevitability or a path from which there is no return. Bottom line: there is a
price to pay for ethical and moral failure. However, given a change in behavior,
the introduction of and application of accountability, and a return to a strong
moral foundation, leaders are able to make ethical and moral decisions.

Principle 4: Ethical and Moral Decision Making is a 360-Degree Process

Organizational decision making may take place in isolation, but the ramifications of those decisions impact more than just the leader. Moreover, the concept of leadership is weakened when isolated from the concept of followership. Although traits and abilities are important elements of most definitions of leadership, one could argue that *influence* is central to what it means to be a leader (Winston & Patterson, 2006).

However, this study reveals that influence is not just about how a leader motivates and inspires followers to work toward organizational goals, it is also about the interplay between multiple external and internal factors and a leader's decision-making process. David was influenced by his past battlefield trauma, the weight or organizational leadership, the environmental uncertainty associated with sociopolitical unrest, and his own lustful desires. These internal and external desires, internal and external stressors, and David's organizational goals and objectives all should have factored into his decision making. However, the evidence suggests that due to the absence of accountability and a forsaking of theologically centered morality, David chose to place the organization at risk by focusing on his own wants and needs. The negative reward of this behavior not only compromised Bathsheba's morality, it also influenced the unethical behavior of Joab. Furthermore, it impacted "David's sons and all of Judea" (Winston, 2016, p. 261). As illustrated in Figure 6, the 360-degree process of ethical and moral decision making requires that one consider all of the internal and external factors that influence a leader's decision-making process. The evidence suggests that leadership fatigue played a critical role in David choosing *self* over others by ignoring the 360-degree nature of the decision-making process.

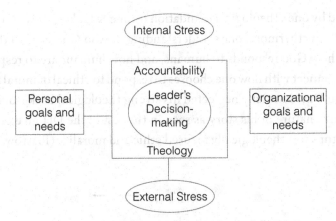

Figure 6: Principle 4—Ethical and moral decision
making is a 360-degree process.

Principle 5: Everything Rises and Falls on Theology

Ethics and morals are "at the heart of life's vital issues" (Rae, 2009, p. 12).
This study centered on a Judeo–Christian framework wherein the Hebrew
and Christian Scriptures are the primary source of all that is truly ethical
and moral. David's behavior was the result of him forsaking his commitment
to God, forsaking his theological understanding of right and wrong, and his
ungodly exploitation of others through a systematic pattern of immorality
and unethical behavior. Since the aforementioned behavior was out of
character in the life and leadership of David, it seems clear that leadership
fatigue damaged David's soul, which ultimately led to a compromised ethical
and moral compass.

   Although 2 Samuel 11 is intentionally ambiguous at times, the heart of
the story conveys a profound truth: God is not pleased with unethical and
immoral behavior. Thus, for the bibliocentric leader, everything rises and
falls on theology. *Everything* includes how one processes stress and trauma.
Theology refers to a "statement (logos) or account about God (theos)"
(Stone & Duke, 2013, "Glossary," para. 47). This study defines theology as
"the process of thinking about, developing, and stating (in words and/or
actions) an understanding of the meaning of faith in the Christian message
of God," it is clear that internal and external stress, the use of accountability/
intermediaries, and the ethical and moral decision-making process are all

impacted by one's theological foundation (Stone & Duke, 2013, "Glossary," para. 47). Furthermore, one's understanding of who God is, who they are to God, how God responds to humans, and how humans are to respond to God all connect with how one chooses to respond to ethical or moral failure. Although David initially neglected his strong theological background, the redemptive nature of his story as seen in the rest of the DH give evidence to his return to a theologically focused ethic and morality (Plastow, 2016).

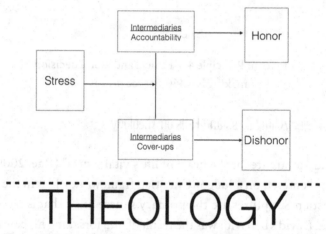

Figure 7: Principle 5—Everything rises and falls on theology.

Figure 7 illustrates how theology is the underpinning for the entire ethical and moral decision-making process. One's theology directly impacts how one processes stress, interacts with intermediaries, and ultimately behaves in response to the multiple variables (Stone & Duke, 2013). Figure 7 illustrates the two basic paths that King David faced in 2 Samuel 11:1-27. Instead of choosing to allow his Mosaic theological foundation to serve as a filter for his stress, David processed the trauma of war, the stress of leadership, and his lust for Bathsheba through an extrabiblical source. David's *theology of self* produced his dishonorable behavior and dishonor toward God (2 Sam. 11:27). The study argues that the converse is also true. If one were to process stress through the Hebrew and Christian Scriptures, submit to accountability as per the Scriptures, and resist temptation as per the Scriptures, then one's theology should produce honorable behavior and honor toward God (Prov 27:17; Gal 6:2; Ephes 5:21; James 1:13-18;). These five principles summarize the lessons learned from 2 Samuel 11. Moreover, these principles provide contemporary leaders with a *way forward* for ethical leadership research and practice. Finally, the principles extrapolated from the passage can be compared with ethical and moral leadership and then further examined for their significance in ecclesial leadership and organizational leadership.

Ethical and Moral Leadership and Leadership Fatigue

There are several connections between the constructs of ethical and moral leadership as outlined in Chapter 2 and David's ethical and moral leadership as seen in 2 Samuel 11. Ethical leadership is a modern construct with ancient roots that connect to a moral underpinning grounded in the moral commands of God as seen in the Hebrew and Christian Scriptures. According to the literature, ethical leadership is linked to multiple contemporary leadership theories such as servant leadership, authentic leadership, spiritual leadership, and transformational leadership (Brown, Treviño et al., 2005; Northouse, 2015; Patterson, 2003; Yukl, 2013). Furthermore, ethical leaders function as *moral managers* who influence the ethical behaviors of their organizations and their followers (Brown & Treviño, 2006).

Although David may have been trying to protect the greater good of Israel by avoiding a public scandal, the evidence suggests that David had a compromised sense of good due to the stress of leadership and a misguided sense of what a leaders should *do* verses who a leader should *be* (Ciulla, 2005). David's misconduct involving Uriah may have stemmed from self-construal-based moral permissibility (Hoyt & Price, 2015). However, there was no *greater good* associated with David's adultery, and God's condemnation of David's activity suggests that David's motives were more than likely self-centered throughout the passage.

Without a doubt, David modeled an unethical way for his followers by choosing ethical egoism over the greater good of the individual and the organization. David's unethical behavior diffused throughout the organization with negative results, thus proving the converse of the Schaubroek et al. (2002) study true. Furthermore, David's behavior confirms Bass' (2009) notion that even the most successful leaders may eventually succumb to unethical leadership, especially when leadership fatigue is allowed to alter one's moral reasoning. David's moral code was compromised not only when he chose to stay in Jerusalem, but also when he allowed the pressure of maintaining a false sense of control to impact his moral judgement (Becker, 2009; Johnson, 2013). In this way, 2 Samuel 11 is an exemplar for how leadership fatigue accelerates moral disengagement and, when left unchecked by accountability, ultimately produces ethical and moral failure in the life of a leader.

Implications

According to Henson (2015), the values and virtues of morality and ethics must continually be developed if leaders are to overcome the lifelong challenges associated with organizational and personal leadership. Therefore, it is important for organizations to develop, implement, and refine their leadership assessment and training processes to account for the role of leadership fatigue on ethical and moral decision making. This is especially true for ecclesial leadership, where the modern ecclesial preparation process tends to focus more on the practical elements of leadership as opposed to the ontological elements of leadership (Crowther 2012b). As mentioned, everything rises and falls on theology. However, many ecclesial organizations have adopted the best business practices of secular organizations in an effort to produce environments of growth and organizational sustainability.

This is not bad in and of itself. However, as evidenced by this study, there is a real if not inevitable danger associated with the pressures of leadership. Leadership fatigue will cloud one's moral reasoning and negatively impact the ethical decision-making process. Therefore, it is paramount that ecclesial leaders be equipped with the tools necessary for regulating leadership fatigue. According to Wilson and Hoffman (2007), most ecclesial leadership failures are not associated with the pragmatics of church leadership. Instead, most ecclesial leadership failure is associated with intimacy, isolation, and a departure from spiritual formation (Wilson & Hoffman, 2007). Thus, the five principles drawn from 2 Samuel 11:1-27 offer ecclesial organizations a series of practical measures that, if implemented, should counter the rising tide of ethical and moral failure amongst ecclesial leaders.

For example, Principle 1 should be taught early and often. According to an examination of three large church-planting organizations, most of the training and development in these organizations centers on the practical side of *how* to do church (Acts 29 Network, 2009, 2015; ARC 2015a, 2015b; CMN, 2007, 2015). However, after the initial assessment phase, it seems as though little training is given on the nature and reality of leadership fatigue. Instead of focusing on rest, counseling, and personal management as a reaction to ethical failure, organizations would do well to take a proactive approach to the stress and trauma of leadership. This study argues that in order to stem the regular occurrences of ecclesial leadership failure, researchers should shift their focus toward the long-term effects of accountability and spiritual formation on ethical and moral decision making and behavior. Thus, it is imperative for researchers to reexamine the training and assessment of ecclesial leaders.

Since accountability is a force multiplier, as stated in Principle 2, organizations should reject the axiom that says "It's lonely at the top" and instead foster a new paradigm wherein leadership is synonymous with accountability, community, and a team (Maxwell, 2007, "Do They Add Value," para. 4). This study is a call for researchers and practitioners to rethink the value of relation intimacy as it relates to accountability in leadership. No one leads in isolation. Moreover, the evidence suggests that there is an inherent value in a leader being accountable to the ethics and morals of his or her followers. Instead of focusing on accountability to a brand or a bottom line, perhaps a new paradigm is in order: accountability to ethics.

Some may function under the assumption that Principle 3 is false. Since leaders often believe that failure is both fatal and final, they often resort to cover-ups or internalizing pressure in a way that negatively impacts the organization and the leader. However, if leaders are given the room to be honest about leadership fatigue and since failure is not final, this newly created *safe space* may foster the transparency necessary for ethical and moral decision-making and behavior.

Therefore, this study calls for researchers to reexamine the negative effects of stigma on honest reporting, especially as it relates to leadership fatigue. The literature clearly has demonstrated that stigma keeps individuals from honestly assessing their mental and emotional state (Blais & Renshaw, 2013). The implications of a renewed effort to counteract stigma in mental health reporting could prove beneficial beyond the confines of ecclesial organizations.

This connects with Principle 4 in that a *culture of transparency* will allow a leader to consider the total scope of his or her ethical and moral decision-making. Finally, ecclesial leaders must never lose sight of their theological foundation. The literature clearly has shown a connection between multiple values-based leadership theories and a biblical theology of leadership (Crowther, 2012b; Henson, 2015; Patterson, 2003). In fact, one could argue that leadership fatigue is inevitable because, theologically speaking, humans were never supposed to lead other humans in the first place.

Principle 5 states that everything rises and falls on theology. According to most Judeo–Christian interpretations of the Scriptures, God intended to lead mankind, while mankind was commissioned to rule over the beasts of the earth (Gen 1:28). However, upon the fall of man and the introduction of sinfulness into the world, God chose to raise up leaders to serve at times as intermediaries between God and humanity. These leaders included family leaders and the rulers of peoples and nations (1 Sam 8:1-9; Prov 8:15; Dan 2:21; Rom 13:1). According to the Protestant Christian worldview, Jesus Christ is both the only intermediary between God and humanity and the leader of the church (Ephes 4:15-16;1 Tim 2:5-6). Nevertheless, the writings and teachings of Luke and the Apostles Paul, Peter, and John contain several instructions for leaders, all of which are applicable in the modern world (Acts 6:1-6; 1 Tim 3:1-13; 2 Tim 2:1-13; Titus 1:5-9). Therefore, ecclesial organizations would do well to remind their leaders that the *weight* of leading other humans is too much for one to bear: Everything rises and falls on theology. This means that during the assessment, training, and development phases, ecclesial leadership training organizations must not be too quick to assume that potential and current leaders are theologically sound. As evidenced in the failure of David in 2 Samuel 11, the first compromise David made was directly linked to theology. Therefore, this study is a call for researchers to once again consider theology as *queen of the sciences* in order to aid in the development of new tools designed to prevent future ethical failure.

Furthermore, this study calls for ecclesial organizations to consider the high cost of ethical and moral failure and then choose to proactively safeguard leaders from the negative impact of leadership fatigue by way of intentional training, accountability, and support. The literature and this study have illustrated that leadership fatigue is a legitimate construct that has an effect on ethical and moral decision making and behavior. The five principles extrapolated from 2 Samuel 11:1-27 not only summarize the findings of the text, they also build upon one another in a way that aids in the prevention of future ethical failure. Since leadership is hard and traumatic, and since accountability is a force multiplier, and since failure is fatal but not final, and since ethical and moral decision making is a 360-degree process, and since everything rises and falls on theology, then it is important for all organizations to move the discussion on ethical leadership beyond theoretical definitions and toward practical steps that will aid in the prevention of future failure and the restoration of those who have already failed.

Limitations of this Study

There are several limitations to consider in this study. The study carefully followed the research methodology outlined in Chapter 3. However, sociorhetorical analysis is only one qualitative method amongst many. Although care was taken to account for the thousands of years of cultural distance between the researcher and the passage, there are theological and vocational biases that cannot be fully overcome within the qualitative research framework. For example, I am a combat veteran who has served in full-time ecclesial leadership for over a decade. However, the rigor of sociorhetorical interpretation and the multidisciplinary approach to the literature protects the validity of this study.

Another limitation of this study is the narrow scope of the sociorhetorical interpretation. Although the study did include multiple references to Scriptures beyond 2 Samuel 11:1-27, critical passages such as 2 Samuel 12:1-31 were not examined on an in-depth level. However, this did not impact the ultimate interpretation of the central passage of the study.

All of the relevant textures of sociorhetorical analysis were utilized in this study. However, it was beyond the scope of this study to offer an in-depth analysis of the multiple values-based leadership theories that connect to ethical and moral leadership. Since King David's leadership has been linked in the literature with charismatic and servant leadership, a more detailed treatment of these theories in the study may have offered more insight into *why* David chose to remain in Jerusalem and why David chose to compound his unethical behavior (Serrano, 2014). Thus, as the first exhaustive study of leadership as seen in 2 Samuel 11:1-27, this study reveals the potential for more research that could come from 2 Samuel 11 and the DH.

The Way Forward

The results, scope, and limitations of this study demonstrate a need for more research into the role of leadership fatigue and its impact on ethical and moral decision making. Although this study proved that leadership principles and practical steps can stem from the systematic exploration of the Hebrew and Christian texts, these principles need further examination. For example, future studies should examine the five principles through other cases of ethical and moral failure found in the Hebrew Scriptures such as in the life of Samson, King Saul, or the various judges and kings of Israel. There is also room to examine these five principles through the lens of Pauline and Petrine ecclesiology, especially since modern Christian ecclesiology follows the constructs of New Testament leadership.

Since the current study is so closely related to the military context, it is important for future studies to explore the five principles in modern military environments such as an active-duty special forces unit. There is also a significant gap in the literature regarding ecclesial leadership in military communities, which could be filled by the aforementioned study. A qualitative study that examines these principles in action may result in a quantitative instrument designed to measure the effectiveness of the principles in preventing future ethical failure.

Finally, it is important for future research to compare the results of this study with current instruments that are designed to measure compassion fatigue, workplace burnout, and PTS. This would not only potentially strengthen the validity of the results of this study, it would also bridge the gap in the literature between ethical leadership and the impact of leadership fatigue on decision making.

CONCLUSION

A Tale of Two Davids

Leadership is hard and traumatic. Leadership fatigue is a real phenomenon that if left unchecked, will take down even the strongest (and smartest) of leaders. It is my hope that these chapters have proven the aforementioned point while also providing a way forward for future leaders and scholars. While speaking to the Senate Armed Services Committee in 2015, David Petraeus sincerely remarked,

> Four years ago, I made a serious mistake—one that brought discredit on me and pain to those closest to me. It was a violation of the trust placed in me and a breach of the values to which I had been committed throughout my life. There is nothing I can do to undo what I did. I can only say again how sorry I am to those I let down and then strive to go forward with a greater sense of humility and purpose, and with gratitude to those who stood with me during a very difficult chapter in my life (Petraeus, 2015).

Two years later, when asked about inner strength and the discipline to overcome obstacles Petraeus said, "We need to learn from our experiences and take responsibilities for our actions and drive on" (Patel, 2017). For a season, King David of Israel lacked humility, lost sight of his purpose, showed disregard for those closest to him, and delayed in taking responsibility for his actions. The similarities between the rise and fall of these two Davids is uncanny. Yet, both Davids eventually recovered and went on to continue leading leaders. Today, David Petraeus serves as the Chairman of the Kohlberg Kravis Roberts and Company (KKR) Global Institute, where he "oversees the Institute's thought leadership platform focused on geopolitical and macroeconomic trends" ("Team," 2017). Moreover, King David of Israel left a lasting legacy of leadership that according to the Christian Scriptures, found its fulfilment in the life of Jesus of Nazareth.

The world needs ethical and moral leaders. The study presented in this book demonstrates that the Hebrew and Christian Scriptures provide a wealth of information that can aid in the creation and sustainment of ethical and moral leaders. Moreover, this study provides organizations with practical solutions to the epidemic of ethical and moral failure across a variety of organizational contexts. By returning to the source of all that is truly moral and ethical, leaders can gain the perspective needed to identify leadership fatigue before it negatively impacts the decision-making process. Furthermore, this study illustrated that although the consequences of ethical and moral failure are often severe, there is always room for redemption in life and leadership.

References

Abasili, A. I. (2011). Was it rape? The David and Bathsheba pericope re-examined. *Vetus Testamentum, 61*(1), 1-15.

Acts 29 Network. (2009). *10 qualifications of a church planter.* Retrieved from http://www.acts29.com/10-qualifications-of-a-church-planter-2/.

Acts 29 Network. (2015). *Why training is important.* Retrieved from http://www.acts29.com/acts-29-training-programs/.

Allen, T. C. (2014). Social media: Pathologists' force multiplier. *Archives of Pathology & Laboratory Medicine, 138*(8), 1000-1001.

Allen, V. L. (2006). *Moral failures of exceptional leaders: A qualitative study* (Doctoral dissertation). Available from ProQuest Dissertations and Theses database. (UMI No. 304922676).

American Psychiatric Association. (2013). *Diagnostic and statistical manual of mental disorders* (5th ed.). Washington, DC: Author.

Andrews, S. J., & Bergen, R. D. (2009). *1, 2 Samuel: Holman Old Testament commentary* (Vol. 6). Nashville, TN: B & H Publishing Group.

ARC. (2015a). *Are you ready to launch a life-giving church?* Retrieved from http://www.arcchurches.com/launch/overview/.

ARC. (2015b). *Give us 2 days and we will show you how to start a life-giving church.* Retrieved from http://www.arcchurches.com/launch/train/.

Avolio, B. J. (2010). *Full range leadership development.* Thousand Oaks, CA: Sage.

Avolio, B. J., & Gardner, W. L. (2005). Authentic leadership development: Getting to the root of positive forms of leadership. *The Leadership Quarterly, 16*(3), 315-338.

Baldwin, J. G. (2008). *1 and 2 Samuel: Tyndale Old Testament commentaries* (Vol. 8). Nottingham, England: InterVarsity Press.

Bandura, A. (1999). Moral disengagement in the perpetration of inhumanities. *Personality and Social Psychology Review, 3*(3), 193-209.

Bass, B. M. (2009). *The Bass handbook of leadership: Theory, research, and managerial applications.* Nashville, TN: Simon and Schuster.

Becker, G. K. (2009). Moral leadership in business. *Journal of International Business Ethics, 2*(1), 7-21.

Beitzel, B. J. (2009). *The New Moody Bible atlas.* Chicago, IL: Moody.

Berger, Y. (2009). Ruth and the David-Bathsheba story: Allusions and contrasts. *Journal for the Study of the Old Testament, 33*(4), 433-452.

Blais, R. K., & Renshaw, K. D. (2013). Stigma and demographic correlates of help-seeking intentions in returning service members. *Journal of Traumatic Stress, 26*(1), 77-85.

Broadwell, P. & Loeb, V. (2012). *All in: The education of General David Petraeus.* London, England: Penguin Press.

Brown, M. E., & Mitchell, M. S. (2010). Ethical and unethical leadership: Exploring new avenues for future research. *Business Ethics Quarterly, 20*(4), 583-616.

Brown, M. E., & Treviño, L. K. (2006). Ethical leadership: A review and future directions. *The Leadership Quarterly, 17*(6), 595-616.

Brown, M., & Treviño, L. (2014). Do role models matter? An investigation of role modeling as an antecedent of perceived ethical leadership. *Journal of Business Ethics, 122*(4), 587-598.

Brown, M. E., Treviño, L. K., & Harrison, D. A. (2005). Ethical leadership: A social learning perspective for construct development and testing. *Organizational Behavior and Human Decision Processes, 97,* 117-134.

Burns, J. M. (1978). *Leadership.* New York, NY: Harper & Row.

Burns, J. M. (2003). *Transforming leadership: A new pursuit of happiness* (Vol. 213). New York, NY: Grove Press.

Camp, P. G. (2011). David's fall: Reading 2 Samuel 11-14 in light of Genesis 2-4. *Restoration Quarterly, 53*(3), 149-158.

Campbell, A. F. (2005). *2 Samuel: The forms of the Old Testament literature* (Vol. VIII). Grand Rapids, MI: Wm. B. Eerdmans.

Campbell, A. F., & O'Brien, M. A. (2000). *Unfolding the Deuteronomistic history: origins, upgrades, present text.* Minneapolis, MN: Fortress Press.

Chamberlin, S. E. (2012). Emasculated by trauma: A social history of post-traumatic stress disorder, stigma, and masculinity. *Journal of American Culture, 35*(4), 358-365.

Ciulla, J. B. (1995). Leadership ethics: Mapping the territory. *Business Ethics Quarterly, 5*(1), 5-28.

Ciulla, J. B. (2005). The state of leadership ethics and the work that lies before us. *Business Ethics: A European Review, 14*(4), 323-335.

CMN. (2007). *Church planting bootcamp journal.* Springfield, MO: Gospel Publishing House.

CMN. (2015). *Assessment.* Retrieved from http://churchmultiplication.net/assessment/.

Collins, B. J. (2007). *The Hittites and their world.* Atlanta, GA: Society of Biblical Literature.

Contractor, A. A., Elhai, J. D., Ractliffe, K. C., & Forbes, D. (2013). PTSD's underlying symptom dimensions and relations with behavioral inhibition and activation. *Journal of Anxiety Disorders, 27,* 645-651.

Conybeare, D., Behar, E., Solomon, A., Newman, M. G., & Borkovec, T. D. (2012). The PTSD checklist-civilian version: Reliability, validity, and factor structure in a nonclinical sample. *Journal of Clinical Psychology, 68*(6), 699-713.

Crowther, S. (2012a). *An examination of leadership principles in 1 Peter in comparison to authentic and kenotic models of leadership* (Doctoral dissertation). Available from ProQuest Dissertations and Theses database. (UMI No. 3515407).

Crowther, S. (2012b). *Peter on leadership: A contemporary exegetical analysis.* Fayetteville, NC: Steven Crowther.

De Cremer, D., Tenbrunsel, A., & Dijke, M. (2010). Regulating ethical failures: Insights from psychology. *Journal of Business Ethics, 95*(1),1-6.

deSilva, D. A. (2004). *An introduction to the New Testament: Contexts, methods, and ministry formation.* Downers Grove, IL: IVP Academic.

Diaconescu, M. (2015). Burnout, secondary trauma and compassion fatigue in social work. *Social Work Review/Revista De Asistenta Sociala, 14*(3), 57-63.

Diestel, S., Cosmar, M., & Schmidt, K. (2013). Burnout and impaired cognitive functioning: The role of executive control in the performance of cognitive tasks. *Work & Stress, 27*(2), 164-180.

DiGangi, J. A., Gomez, D., Mendoza, L., Jason, L. A., Keys, C. B., & Koenen, K. C. (2013). Pretrauma risk factors for posttraumatic stress disorder: A systematic review of the literature. *Clinical Psychology Review, 33,* 728-744.

Finkelstein, I., & Silberman, N. A. (2007). *David and Solomon: In search of the Bible's sacred kings and the roots of the western tradition.* New York, NY: Simon and Schuster.

Floyd, S. (2008). *Crisis counseling: A guide for pastors and professionals.* Grand Rapids, MI: Kregel Academic and Professional.

Fluker, W. E. (2009). *Ethical leadership: The quest for character, civility, and community.* Minneapolis, MN: Fortress Press.

Forward, G. L. (2000). Clergy stress and role metaphors: An exploratory study. *Journal of Communication & Religion, 23*(2), 158-184.

Fry, L. W. (2003). Toward a theory of spiritual leadership. *The Leadership Quarterly, 14*(6), 93-727.

Gabriel, R. A. (2003). *The military history of ancient Israel.* Westport, CT: Greenwood Publishing Group.

Garsiel, M. (1993). The story of David and Bathsheba: A different approach. *Catholic Biblical Quarterly, 55*(2), 244-262.

Gerhart, M. (1989). The restoration of biblical narrative. *Semeia, 46,* 13-29.

Gordon, R. P. (1999). *I & II Samuel: A commentary.* Grand Rapids, MI: Zondervan.

Greenberg, G. (2003). *Sins of King David.* Naperville, IL: Sourcebooks.

Grosch, W. N., & Olsen, D. C. (2000). Clergy burnout: An integrative approach. *Journal of Clinical Psychology, 56*(5), 619-632.

Grossman, D. (2009). *On killing: The psychological cost of learning to kill in war and society.* New York, NY: Back Bay Books.

Grossman, D., & Christensen, L. W. (2012). *On combat: The psychology and physiology of deadly conflict in war and in peace.* Belleville, IL: PPCT Research Publications.

Harman, R., & Lee, D. (2010). The role of shame and self-critical thinking in the development and maintenance of current threat in post-traumatic stress disorder. *Clinical Psychology & Psychotherapy, 17*(1), 13-24.

Hauer, C. E. (1978). David's army. *Concordia Journal, 4*(2), 68-72.

Hendron, J., Irving, P., & Taylor, B. (2012). The unseen cost: A discussion of the secondary traumatization experience of the clergy. *Pastoral Psychology, 61*(2), 221-231.

Hendron, J. A., Irving, P., & Taylor, B. J. (2014). Clergy stress through working with trauma: A qualitative study of secondary impact. *Journal of Pastoral Care & Counseling* (Online), 68(4), 1-14.

Henson, J. D. (2015). *An examination of the role of spirituality in the development of the moral component of authentic leadership through a sociorhetorical analysis of Paul's letter to Titus* (Doctoral dissertation). Available from Dissertations and Theses database. (UMI No. 3682828).

Hernando, J. D. (2005). *Dictionary of hermeneutics: A concise guide to terms, names, methods, and expressions.* Springfield, MO: Gospel Publishing House.

Hertzberg, H. W. (1965). *I and II Samuel: A commentary.* Louisville, KY: Westminster John Knox Press.

House, R. J., & Aditya, R. N. (1997). The social scientific study of leadership: Quo vadis? *Journal of Management, 23*(3), 409-473.

Hoyt, C. L., & Price, T. L. (2015). Ethical decision making and leadership: Merging social role and self-construal perspectives. *Journal of Business Ethics, 126*(4), 531-539.

Huizing, R. L. (2013). *The importance of ritual for follower development: An intertexture analysis of Leviticus 23 in the Pauline corpus* (Doctoral dissertation). Available from ProQuest Dissertations and Theses database. (UMI No. 3570908).

Jaffe, A. E., DiLillo, D., Hoffman, L., Haikalis, M., & Dykstra, R. E. (2015). Does it hurt to ask? A meta-analysis of participant reactions to trauma research. *Clinical Psychology Review, 40*, 40-56.

Johnson, C. E. (2013). *Meeting the ethical challenges of leadership: Casting light or shadow.* Thousand Oaks, CA: Sage.

Kanungo, R. N., & Mendonca, M. (1996). *Ethical dimensions of leadership* (Vol. 3). Thousand Oaks, CA: Sage.

Kim, U. (2002). Uriah the Hittite: A (con)text of struggle for identity. *Semeia, 90/91*, 69-85.

KKR (2017). *Team.* Retrieved from http://www.kkr.com/our-firm/leadership/david-h-petraeus.

Koffel, E., Polusny, M. A., Arbisi, P. A., & Erbes, C. R. (2012). A preliminary investigation of the new and revised symptoms of posttraumatic stress disorder in DSM-5. *Depression and Anxiety, 29*(8), 731-738.

Kouzes, J. M., & Posner, B. Z. (2006). *The leadership challenge* (Vol. 3). Hoboken, NJ: John Wiley & Sons.

Ludwig, D. C., & Longenecker, C. O. (1993). The Bathsheba syndrome: The ethical failure of successful leaders. *Journal of Business Ethics, 12*(4), 265-273.

Maslach, C., Schaufeli, W. B., & Leiter, M. P. (2001). Job burnout. *Annual Review of Psychology, 52,* 397 422.

Maxwell, J. C. (2007). *The 21 irrefutable laws of leadership: Follow them and people will follow you.* Nashville, TN: Thomas Nelson.

Meadors, G. T., & Kaiser, W. C. (Eds.). (2009). *Four views on moving beyond the Bible to theology.* Grand Rapids, MI: Zondervan.

Merrill, E. H., Rooker, M. F., & Grisanti, M. A. (2011). *The world and the word: An introduction to the Old Testament.* Nashville, TN: B&H.

Midgen, T. (2015). (Un)Ethical leadership: What can educational psychology services learn? *Educational & Child Psychology, 32*(4), 81-93.

Na'aman, N. (1988). The list of David's officers (šālišim). *Vetus Testamentum, 38*(1), 71-79.

Nelson-Jones, R. (1981). *The double redaction of the Deuteronomistic history.* Sheffield, England: Sheffield Academic Press.

Noth, M. (1958). *The history of Israel.* New York, NY: Harper.

Noth, M. (1981). *The Deuteronomistic history* (Vol. 15). Sheffield, England: Sheffield Academic Press.

Noth, M. (1987). *The chronicler's history* (Vol. 50). Sheffield, England: Sheffield Academic Press.

Northouse, P. G. (2015). *Leadership: Theory and practice.* Thousand Oaks, CA: Sage.

Osborne, G. A. (2006). *The hermeneutical spiral: A comprehensive introduction to biblical interpretation.* Westmont, IL: IVP.

Oswalt, J. N. (2009). *The Bible among the myths: Unique revelation or just ancient literature?* Grand Rapids, MI: Zondervan.

Patel, D. (2017). *Gen. David Petraeus: Career advice from a former CIA director.* Retrieved from https://deeppatel.com/gen-david-petraeus-career-advice-from-a-former-cia-director/.

Patterson, K. A. (2003). *Servant leadership: A theoretical model* (Doctoral dissertation). Available from ProQuest Dissertations and Theses database. (UMI No. 3082719).

Patton, M. Q. (2002). *Qualitative research & evaluation methods.* Thousand Oaks, CA: Sage.

Peckham, B. (1985). *The composition of the Deuteronomistic history* (Vol. 35). Atlanta, GA: Scholars Pr.

Perry, A. (2016). *Exemplary lives in speech, conduct, love, faith, and purity: An analysis of 1 Timothy 3-4 for ethical leadership* (Doctoral dissertation). Available from ProQuest Dissertations and Theses database. (UMI No. 3745410).

Peterson, B. N. (2014). *The Authors of the Deuteronomistic history: Locating a tradition in ancient Israel.* Minneapolis, MN: Fortress Press.

Petraeus, D.H. (2015). *Testimony prepared for the senate armed services committee U.S. policy in the middle east.* Retrieved from https://www. armed-services.senate.gov/imo/media/doc/Petraeus_09-22-15.pdf.

Plastow, J. (2016). Breaking points: What today's leaders can learn from King David's failure and response. In B. E. Winston & K. Patterson (Eds.), *Ethics: The Old Testament, the New Testament, and contemporary application* (pp. 195-209). North Charleston, SC: Create Space Independent Publishing Platform.

Rae, S. B. (2009). *Moral choices: An introduction to ethics.* Grand Rapids, MI: Zondervan Academic.

Regel, S., & Joseph, S. (2010). *Post-traumatic stress.* New York, NY: Oxford University Press.

Reger, G. M., Durham, T. L., Tarantino, K. A., Luxton, D. D., Holloway, K. M., & Lee, J. A. (2013). Deployed soldiers' reactions to exposure and medication treatments for PTSD. *Psychological Trauma: Theory, Research, Practice, and Policy, 5*(4), 309-316.

Reese, E. (1994). *The Reese chronological bible: King James version.* Bloomington, MN: Bethany House.

Rhode, D. L. (2006). *Moral leadership: The theory and practice of power, judgment and policy* (Vol. 139). Hoboken, NJ: John Wiley & Sons.

Robbins, V. K. (1996a). *Exploring the texture of texts: A guide to socio-rhetorical interpretation.* New York, NY: Bloomsbury Press.

Robbins, V. K. (1996b). *The tapestry of early Christian discourse: Rhetoric, society, and ideology.* New York, NY: Routledge.

Robbins, V. K. (1999). *Socio-rhetorical interpretation from its beginning to the present.* Retrieved from http://www.religion.emory.edu/faculty/ robbins/ Pdfs/SNTSPretSocRhetfromBeginning.pdf.

Robbins, V. K. (2004). *Beginnings and developments in socio-rhetorical interpretation.* Retrieved from http://www.religion.emory.edu /faculty/ robbins/Pdfs/SRIBegDevRRA.pdf.

Robbins, V. K. (2008). Rhetography: A new way of seeing the familiar text. In C. C. Black & D. F. Watson (Eds), *Words well spoken: George Kennedy's rhetoric of the New Testament* (pp. 81-105). Waco, TX: Baylor University Press.

Römer, T. (2007). *The so-called Deuteronomistic history: A sociological, historical and literary introduction.* New York, NY: Bloomsbury-T&T Clark.

Rosenberg, J. (1989). The institutional matrix of treachery in 2 Samuel 11. *Semeia, 46,* 103-116.

Ross, W. A. (2015). The authors of the Deuteronomistic history: Locating a tradition in ancient Israel. *Journal of the Evangelical Theological Society, 58*(2), 376-378.

Ruthven, P., & Ruthven, J. (2001). The feckless later reign of King David: A case of major depressive disorder? *The Journal of Pastoral Care, 55*(4), 425-432.

Schaubroek, J. M., Hannah, S. T., Avolio, B. J., Kozlowski, S. W., Lord, R. G., Treviño, L. K., ... Peng, A. C. (2002). Embedding ethical leadership within and across organizational levels. *Academy of Management Journal, 55*(5), 1053-1078.

Schuh, S. C., Zhang, X. A., & Tian, P. (2013). For the good or the bad? Interactive effects of transformational leadership with moral and authoritarian leadership behaviors. *Journal of Business Ethics, 116*(3), 629-640.

Serrano, C. (2014). Charismatic and servant leadership as seen in King Saul and young David: An inner texture analysis of 1 Samuel 17:1-58. *Journal of Biblical Perspectives in Leadership, 6*(1), 27-40.

Skogstad, M., Skorstad, M., Lie, A., Conradi, H. S., Heir, T., & Weisæth, L. (2013). Work-related post-traumatic stress disorder. *Occupational Medicine, 63*(3), 175-182.

Sternberg, M. (1987). *The poetics of biblical narrative: Ideological literature and the drama of reading.* Bloomington: Indiana University Press.

Stevens, M. E. (2012). *Leadership roles of the Old Testament: King, prophet, priest.* Thousand Oaks, CA: Sage.

Stone, H. W., & Duke, J. O. (2013). *How to think theologically.* Minneapolis, MN: Fortress Press.

Sundin, J., Fear, N. T., Iversen, A., Rona, R. J., & Wessely, S. (2010). PTSD after deployment to Iraq: Conflicting rates, conflicting claims. *Psychological Medicine, 40*(3), 367-382.

Tanner, M., Wherry, J., & Zvonkovic, A. (2013). Clergy who experience trauma as a result of forced termination. *Journal of Religion & Health, 52*(4), 1281-1295.

Thistle, B. M., & Molinaro, V. (2016). Driving organizational transformation through strong leadership accountability: It's time for HR leaders to step up. *People & Strategy, 39*(3), 28-31.

Tichy, N. M., & McGill, A. (2003). *The ethical challenge: How to lead with unyielding integrity* (Vol. 31). Hoboken, NJ: John Wiley & Sons.

Tick, E. (2012). *War and the soul: Healing our nation's veterans from post-traumatic stress disorder.* Wheaton, IL: Quest Books.

Tick, E. (2014). *Warrior's return: Restoring the soul after war.* Louisville, CO: Sounds True.

Translation Philosophy. (2015). Retrieved from http://www.esv.org/about/translation-philosophy/.

U.S. Joint Chiefs of Staff. (2014, July 16). *Joint publication 3-05: Special operations.* Retrieved from http://www.dtic.mil/doctrine/new_pubs/jp3_05.pdf.

Vanhoozer, K. J. (2009). *Is there a meaning in this text? The Bible, the reader and the morality of literary knowledge.* Grand Rapids, MI: Zondervan.

Walton, J. (2006). *Ancient Near Eastern thought and the Old Testament: Introducing the conceptual world of the Hebrew Bible.* Ada, MI: Baker Academic.

Williams, J. J., & Allen, S. A. (2015). Trauma-inspired prosocial leadership development. *Journal of Leadership Education, 14*(3), 86-103.

Willimon, W. H. (1993). A peculiarly Christian account of sin. *Theology Today, 50*(2), 220-228.

Wilson, M. T., & Hoffmann, B. (2007). *Preventing ministry failure: A shepherd care guide for pastors, ministers and other caregivers.* Downers Grove, IL: IVP Books.

Winston, B. E. (2016). Conclusion—Lessons learned. In B. E. Winston & K. Patterson (Eds), *Ethics: The Old Testament, the New Testament, and contemporary application* (pp. 195-209). North Charleston, SC: Create Space Independent Publishing Platform.

Winston, B. E., & Patterson, K. (2006). An integrative definition of leadership. *International Journal of Leadership Studies, 1*(2), 6-66.

Yee, G. A. (1988). "Fraught with background": Literary ambiguity in 2 Samuel 11. *Interpretation, 42*(3), 240-253.

Yukl, G. A. (2013). *Leadership in organizations* (7th ed.). Upper Saddle River, NJ: Pearson Education.

Youngblood, R. F. (1992). *The expositor's Bible commentary—1 & 2 Samuel.* Grand Rapids, MI: Zondervan.

Zheng, D., Witt, L., Waite, E., David, E. M., van Driel, M., McDonald, D. P., & Crepeau, L. J. (2015). Effects of ethical leadership on emotional exhaustion in high moral intensity situations. *The Leadership Quarterly, 26*(5), 732-748.

APPENDIX A
List of Abbreviations

ANE	Ancient Near East
DH	Deuteronomist History
Dtr	The Deuteronomist
Dtr^1	Josianic Deuteronomist
Dtr^2	Exilic Deuteronomist
DSM-IV/DSM-5	*Diagnostic and Statistical Manual of Mental Disorders* 4 and 5
E	The Elohist narrative
J	The Yahwistic narrative
P	The priestly narratives
PTS	Posttraumatic stress
PTSD	Posttraumatic stress disorder
PCL-C	PTSD Checklist-Civilian Version
MDD	Major depressive disorder
U.S.	United States

For more information please visit http://www.morethanwordsllc.com/

H&S

COACHING AND CONSULTING

Helping you move forward.

We believe that healthy leaders should be in the business of leading their businesses instead of *running* everything. We believe that healthy people should lead themselves instead of *running* all over the place. We help you move forward by providing solutions to whatever has you stuck. That way, you can do what only you can do...lead. We are committed to helping you navigate this thing called life. From learning how to maximize your time and resources to re-thinking your organizational structure and systems, we can help you discover where you are and provide you with the tools to move forward. For more information please visit http://hoskinsserrano.com/

About the Author

Carlo Serrano is an experienced business growth consultant, speaker, and researcher. Much of his work focuses on organizational health and growth in military communities. He has over 12 years of experience in non-profit executive leadership. He is a published researcher with work related to leadership emergence and servant leadership. Along with serving as managing partner of H&S Coaching and Consulting, he is the Teaching Pastor of oneChurch.tv in Clarksville, TN and an Adjunct Professor at multiple colleges and universities. Carlo has a Ph.D. in  Organizational Leadership from Regent University. He received his M.A. in Pastoral Counseling from Liberty University and his B.A. in Psychology from American Military University. Carlo and his wife Jaemi have two sons. He is passionate about reading, the Beatles, and training Brazilian Jiu Jitsu.

Printed in the United States
By Bookmasters

Printed in the United States
By Bookmasters